THE
CHEROKEE

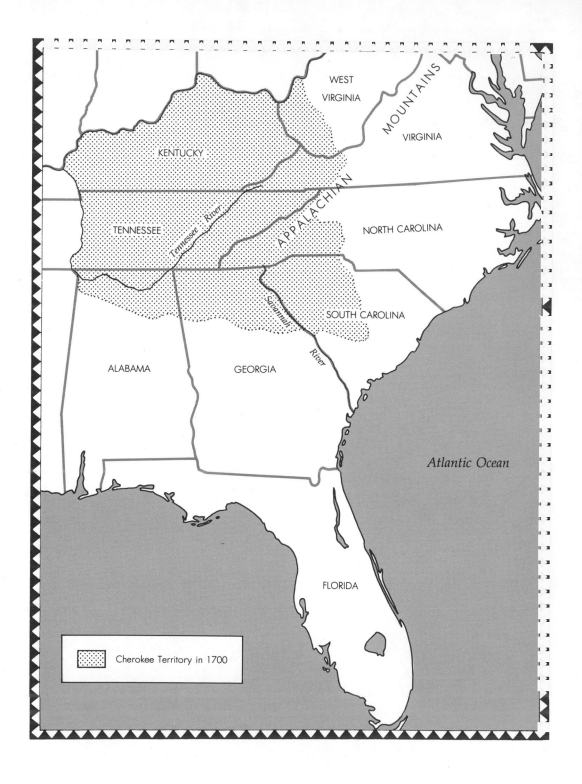

WEST
VIRGINIA

VIRGINIA

MOUNTAINS

KENTUCKY

TENNESSEE

Tennessee River

APPALACHIAN

NORTH CAROLINA

SOUTH CAROLINA

Savannah River

ALABAMA

GEORGIA

Atlantic Ocean

FLORIDA

Cherokee Territory in 1700

THE
CHEROKEE

Theda Perdue
University of Kentucky

Frank W. Porter III
General Editor

CHELSEA HOUSE PUBLISHERS
New York   Philadelphia

On the cover A Cherokee basket, woven of straw.

Chelsea House Publishers
Editor-in-Chief Nancy Toff
Executive Editor Remmel T. Nunn
Managing Editor Karyn Gullen Browne
Copy Chief Juliann Barbato
Picture Editor Adrian G. Allen
Art Director Maria Epes
Manufacturing Manager Gerald Levine

Indians of North America
Senior Editor Sam Tanenhaus

Staff for **THE CHEROKEE**
Associate Editor Abigail Meisel
Deputy Copy Chief Ellen Scordato
Editorial Assistant Tara P. Deal, Clark Morgan
Assistant Art Director Laurie Jewell
Senior Designer Victoria Tomaselli
Picture Researcher Ed Dixon, Amla Sanghvi
Production Coordinator Joseph Romano

3 5 7 9 8 6 4

Library of Congress Cataloging in Publication Data

Perdue, Theda, 1949–
The Cherokee / Theda Perdue.
    p.   cm.—(Indians of North America)
Bibliography: p.
Includes index.
ISBN 1-55546-695-8
        0-7910-0357-4 (pbk.)
1. Cherokee Indians. I. Title.   II. Series: Indians of North
America (Chelsea House Publishers)
E99.C5P393   1988   88-14175
973'.0497—dc 19   CIP

CONTENTS

Indians of North America:
Conflict and Survival   7
by Frank W. Porter III

1. The Principal People   13
2. Cherokees and Europeans   27
3. Cherokee "Civilization"   39
4. Removal   49
5. The Cherokees in the West   61

   Picture Essay
   The Enduring Legacy of Cherokee Crafts   65

6. The Eastern Band of Cherokees   83
7. Cherokees in the 20th Century   93

   Bibliography   104
   The Cherokee at a Glance   105
   Glossary   106
   Index   107

INDIANS OF NORTH AMERICA

The Abenaki

American Indian
Literature

The Apache

The Arapaho

The Archaeology
of North America

The Aztecs

The Cahuilla

The Catawbas

The Cherokee

The Cheyenne

The Chickasaw

The Chinook

The Chipewyan

The Choctaw

The Chumash

The Coast Salish Peoples

The Comanche

The Creeks

The Crow

The Eskimo

Federal Indian Policy

The Hidatsa

The Huron

The Iroquois

The Kiowa

The Kwakiutl

The Lenapes

The Lumbee

The Maya

The Menominee

The Modoc

The Montagnais-Naskapi

The Nanticoke

The Narragansett

The Navajo

The Nez Perce

The Ojibwa

The Osage

The Paiute

The Pima-Maricopa

The Potawatomi

The Powhatan Tribes

The Pueblo

The Quapaw

The Seminole

The Tarahumara

The Tunica-Biloxi

Urban Indians

The Wampanoag

Women in American
Indian Society

The Yakima

The Yankton Sioux

The Yuma

CHELSEA HOUSE PUBLISHERS

INDIANS OF NORTH AMERICA: CONFLICT AND SURVIVAL

Frank W. Porter III

*The Indians survived our
open intention of wiping them
out, and since the tide turned
they have even weathered
our good intentions toward them,
which can be much more deadly.*

John Steinbeck
America and Americans

When Europeans first reached the North American continent, they found hundreds of tribes occupying a vast and rich country. The newcomers quickly recognized the wealth of natural resources. They were not, however, so quick or willing to recognize the spiritual, cultural, and intellectual riches of the people they called Indians.

The Indians of North America examines the problems that develop when people with different cultures come together. For American Indians, the consequences of their interaction with non-Indian people have been both productive and tragic. The Europeans believed they had "discovered" a "New World," but their religious bigotry, cultural bias, and materialistic world view kept them from appreciating and understanding the people who lived in it. All too often they attempted to change the way of life of the indigenous people. The Spanish conquistadores wanted the Indians as a source of labor. The Christian missionaries, many of whom were English, viewed them as potential converts. French traders and trappers used the Indians as a means to obtain pelts. As Francis Parkman, the 19th-century historian, stated, "Spanish civilization crushed the Indian; English civilization scorned and neglected him; French civilization embraced and cherished him."

Nearly 500 years later, many people think of American Indians as curious vestiges of a distant past, waging a futile war to survive in a Space Age society. Even today, our understanding of the history and culture of American Indians is too often derived from unsympathetic, culturally biased, and inaccurate reports. The American Indian, described and portrayed in thousands of movies, television programs, books, articles, and government studies, has either been raised to the status of the "noble savage" or disparaged as the "wild Indian" who resisted the westward expansion of the American frontier.

7

Where in this popular view are the real Indians, the human beings and communities whose ancestors can be traced back to ice-age hunters? Where are the creative and indomitable people whose sophisticated technologies used the natural resources to ensure their survival, whose military skill might even have prevented European settlement of North America if not for devastating epidemics and the disruption of the ecology? Where are the men and women who are today diligently struggling to assert their legal rights and express once again the value of their heritage?

The various Indian tribes of North America, like people everywhere, have a history that includes population expansion, adaptation to a range of regional environments, trade across wide networks, internal strife, and warfare. This was the reality. Europeans justified their conquests, however, by creating a mythical image of the New World and its native people. In this myth, the New World was a virgin land, waiting for the Europeans. The arrival of Christopher Columbus ended a timeless primitiveness for the original inhabitants.

Also part of this myth was the debate over the origins of the American Indians. Fantastic and diverse answers were proposed by the early explorers, missionaries, and settlers. Some thought that the Indians were descended from the Ten Lost Tribes of Israel, others that they were descended from inhabitants of the lost continent of Atlantis. One writer suggested that the Indians had reached North America in another Noah's ark.

A later myth, perpetrated by many historians, focused on the relentless persecution during the past five centuries until only a scattering of these "primitive" people remained to be herded onto reservations. This view fails to chronicle the overt and covert ways in which the Indians successfully coped with the intruders.

All of these myths presented one-sided interpretations that ignored the complexity of European and American events and policies. All left serious questions unanswered. What were the origins of the American Indians? Where did they come from? How and when did they get to the New World? What was their life—their culture—really like?

In the late 1800s, anthropologists and archaeologists in the Smithsonian Institution's newly created Bureau of American Ethnology in Washington, D. C., began to study scientifically the history and culture of the Indians of North America. They were motivated by an honest belief that the Indians were on the verge of extinction and that along with them would vanish their languages, religious beliefs, technology, myths, and legends. These men and women went out to visit, study, and record data from as many Indian communities as possible before this information was forever lost.

By this time there was a new myth in the national consciousness. American Indians existed as figures in the American past. They had performed a historical mission. They had challenged white settlers who trekked across the continent. Once conquered, however, they were supposed to accept graciously the way of life of their conquerors.

The reality again was different. American Indians resisted both actively and passively. They refused to lose their unique identity, to be assimilated into white society. Many whites viewed the Indians not only as members of a conquered nation but also as "inferior" and "unequal." The rights of the Indians could be expanded, contracted, or modified as the conquerors saw fit. In every generation, white society asked itself what to do with the American Indians. Their answers have resulted in the twists and turns of federal Indian policy.

There were two general approaches. One way was to raise the Indians to a "higher level" by "civilizing" them. Zealous missionaries considered it their Christian duty to elevate the Indian through conversion and scanty education. The other approach was to ignore the Indians until they disappeared under pressure from the ever-expanding white society. The myth of the "vanishing Indian" gave stronger support to the latter option, helping to justify the taking of the Indians' land.

Prior to the end of the 18th century, there was no national policy on Indians simply because the American nation had not yet come into existence. American Indians similarly did not possess a political or social unity with which to confront the various Europeans. They were not homogeneous. Rather, they were loosely formed bands and tribes, speaking nearly 300 languages and thousands of dialects. The collective identity felt by Indians today is a result of their common experiences of defeat and/or mistreatment at the hands of whites.

During the colonial period, the British crown did not have a coordinated policy toward the Indians of North America. Specific tribes (most notably the Iroquois and the Cherokee) became military and political pawns used by both the crown and the individual colonies. The success of the American Revolution brought no immediate change. When the United States acquired new territory from France and Mexico in the early 19th century, the federal government wanted to open this land to settlement by homesteaders. But the Indian tribes that lived on this land had signed treaties with European governments assuring their title to the land. Now the United States assumed legal responsibility for honoring these treaties.

At first, President Thomas Jefferson believed that the Louisiana Purchase contained sufficient land for both the Indians and the white population.

9

Within a generation, though, it became clear that the Indians would not be allowed to remain. In the 1830s the federal government began to coerce the eastern tribes to sign treaties agreeing to relinquish their ancestral land and move west of the Mississippi River. Whenever these negotiations failed, President Andrew Jackson used the military to remove the Indians. The southeastern tribes, promised food and transportation during their removal to the West, were instead forced to walk the "Trail of Tears." More than 4,000 men, women, and children died during this forced march. The "removal policy" was successful in opening the land to homesteaders, but it created enormous hardships for the Indians.

By 1871 most of the tribes in the United States had signed treaties ceding most or all of their ancestral land in exchange for reservations and welfare. The treaty terms were intended to bind both parties for all time. But in the General Allotment Act of 1887, the federal government changed its policy again. Now the goal was to make tribal members into individual landowners and farmers, encouraging their absorption into white society. This policy was advantageous to whites who were eager to acquire Indian land, but it proved disastrous for the Indians. One hundred thirty-eight million acres of reservation land were subdivided into tracts of 160, 80, or as little as 40 acres, and allotted to tribe members on an individual basis. Land owned in this way was said to have "trust status" and could not be sold. But the surplus land—all Indian land not allotted to individuals— was opened (for sale) to white settlers. Ultimately, more than 90 million acres of land were taken from the Indians by legal and illegal means.

The resulting loss of land was a catastrophe for the Indians. It was necessary to make it illegal for Indians to sell their land to non-Indians. The Indian Reorganization Act of 1934 officially ended the allotment period. Tribes that voted to accept the provisions of this act were reorganized, and an effort was made to purchase land within preexisting reservations to restore an adequate land base.

Ten years later, in 1944, federal Indian policy again shifted. Now the federal government wanted to get out of the "Indian business." In 1953 an act of Congress named specific tribes whose trust status was to be ended "at the earliest possible time." This new law enabled the United States to end unilaterally, whether the Indians wished it or not, the special status that protected the land in Indian tribal reservations. In the 1950s federal Indian policy was to transfer federal responsibility and jurisdiction to state governments, encourage the physical relocation of Indian peoples from reservations to urban areas, and hasten the termination, or extinction, of tribes.

Between 1954 and 1962 Congress passed specific laws authorizing the termination of more than 100 tribal groups. The stated purpose of the termination policy was to ensure the full and complete integration of Indians into American society. However, there is a less benign way to interpret this legislation. Even as termination was being discussed in Congress, 133 separate bills were introduced to permit the transfer of trust land ownership from Indians to non-Indians.

With the Johnson administration in the 1960s the federal government began to reject termination. In the 1970s yet another Indian policy emerged. Known as "self-determination," it favored keeping the protective role of the federal government while increasing tribal participation in, and control of, important areas of local government. In 1983 President Reagan, in a policy statement on Indian affairs, restated the unique "government to government" relationship of the United States with the Indians. However, federal programs since then have moved toward transferring Indian affairs to individual states, which have long desired to gain control of Indian land and resources.

As long as American Indians retain power, land, and resources that are coveted by the states and the federal government, there will continue to be a "clash of cultures," and the issues will be contested in the courts, Congress, the White House, and even in the international human rights community. To give all Americans a greater comprehension of the issues and conflicts involving American Indians today is a major goal of this series. These issues are not easily understood, nor can these conflicts be readily resolved. The study of North American Indian history and culture is a necessary and important step toward that comprehension. All Americans must learn the history of the relations between the Indians and the federal government, recognize the unique legal status of the Indians, and understand the heritage and cultures of the Indians of North America.

A Cherokee girl poses in ceremonial dress, including headdress and necklaces, near the turn of the century.

THE PRINCIPAL PEOPLE

The Cherokees called themselves "Ani'-Yun'wiya," the principal people. They lived in a land of high mountains and green valleys, today called the southern Appalachians. The Cherokees believed that their homeland was in the center of the world and pictured the earth as a floating island suspended by four cords from the sky, which was made of solid rock. Before the island was created, everyone lived above the rock sky, where it was very crowded. The water beetle went down to explore the vast sea beneath the sky. He found no land, but he dived below the water and surfaced with mud that began to grow until it formed the island of the earth. The water beetle returned to the sky and the buzzard went down to see if the island was dry enough for the animals. The buzzard became tired, and his wings began to hit the ground. Everywhere his wings struck the earth, which was still soft, there was a valley, and when he lifted them he made a mountain. This is why the Cherokee country is covered with mountains.

At last the earth was dry enough for plants and animals to come down from the sky. They tried to stay awake, but most soon went to sleep. The owl, panther, and a few other animals managed to stay awake for seven days, and as a result they acquired the power to see in the dark and hunt animals that sleep. Of the plants, the pine, cedar, spruce, holly, and laurel stayed awake. This is why they stay green year-round instead of losing their leaves in winter like the plants who slept.

The first man and woman were called Kana'ti and Selu. They had only one son until a mysterious child whom they called "Wild Boy" sprang from the river where Selu had washed game. They captured him and tried to tame him, but he remained mischievous.

Kana'ti provided meat for the family. He never failed to bring home deer or turkey when he went hunting in the mountains. One day the two boys followed their father to see how he had such good luck. He went into the swamp, cut some reeds, and made arrows. Then he climbed a mountainside until he reached a large rock. When he lifted the rock, a fat buck ran out and Kana'ti shot the animal with his arrows.

Several days later, the boys tried to imitate their father. They made arrows and went to the mountain where Kana'ti killed the game. They lifted the rock, and a deer ran out. They were not quick and skillful like Kana'ti, and before they could shoot that deer, another ran out. In their confusion, they forgot to replace the rock, and all the game escaped. When Kana'ti found out what they had done, he went into the cave where he found only jars of fleas, lice, bedbugs, gnats, and other vermin. These he released on the boys to punish them. From that day, Kana'ti had to look for game all over the woods. Sometimes he found food, but sometimes his family had to go hungry.

Selu provided vegetables for the family. She always got corn and beans from the storehouse. One day the boys spied on her when she went there. They saw her stand in front of a basket rubbing her stomach; suddenly corn appeared in the basket. Then she rubbed her armpits, and beans filled the basket. The boys were horrified: Their mother, they decided, was a witch and they must kill her!

Selu knew their intentions. Before she died, she told them to clear the land in front of the cabin, drag her body around the clearing seven times, and stay awake all night. Then there would be plenty of corn in the morning. Be-

cause the boys were lazy, they only cleared seven little spots, and they dragged their mother's body over the ground only twice. As a result, corn grew in only a few spots and required cultivation.

The stories about the island and about Kana'ti and Selu were recorded in the late 1800s by anthropologist James Mooney, who visited Cherokees living in North Carolina. The Cherokees told Mooney that these myths had existed for hundreds of years. They were far more than children's stories; although most Cherokees probably learned them as children these myths explained why Cherokees lived as they did. All peoples develop explanations for how the world was made, how plants and animals acquired their particular characteristics, how the first people lived, and how their own society came into being. The myths Mooney wrote down explained how the principal people's world had developed.

For the Cherokees, the mountains that the buzzard made had been their home for at least a thousand years when Europeans first arrived in their villages in 1540. Western North Carolina was the heart of the Cherokee homeland but in the early years of European contact they also lived in what is today up-country South Carolina, northern Georgia, northeastern Alabama, and eastern Tennessee.

The Cherokees lived in villages that sometimes stretched for several miles along riverbanks. Each village had a council house (or town house) and a plaza where the villagers met to socialize, make political decisions, and conduct religious ceremonies. The council house was a very large circular building that sometimes sat atop an earthen mound. The walls of the council house were constructed of wattle (a fabrication of interwoven saplings) and then covered with daub (a plasterlike substance made with mud). Benches lined the walls, and a fire smoldered in a central hearth. There were no windows and only a small opening for a door. The council house opened onto a plaza that was surrounded by covered sheds, where villagers sat during warm summer weather to watch events such as games, dances, and ceremonies.

Beyond the council house and plaza lay private houses. A Cherokee household was large: It often included several generations. Therefore, Cherokee homesteads consisted of several buildings. In summer Cherokees lived in large, rectangular, clapboard houses. In winter they moved into their *asi* (winter houses), which were small, round, wattle-and-daub structures. The fire constantly smoldering in the hearth made the windowless asi dark and smoky. Households also had storage buildings

The Cherokee homeland in the Appalachian Mountains of North Carolina. According to ancient Cherokee beliefs, the homeland was in the center of the world.

Statues excavated from Cherokee territory in northern Georgia represent Kana'ti, the first man (left), and Selu, the first woman—the mythical ancestors of the Cherokee.

the cornstalks and the nitrogen naturally produced by beans fertilized the corn. Between these hills, they grew squash, sunflowers, pumpkins, and other crops.

Like Selu, women were responsible for providing vegetables. Men might help with clearing fields, planting, and harvesting, but the chief responsibility for agriculture fell to the women. They hoed the crops with stone implements or pointed digging sticks. Old women, who could not perform such heavy physical labor, helped by sitting on scaffolds in the middle of fields and chasing away crows and raccoons that tried to raid the crops. When the corn was edible, the women presented it to the village in the Cherokees' most important ritual, the Green Corn Ceremony.

While they were busy in the fields, women also had to tend to their children. Because they lived in extended families, which included several mothers with children of different ages as well as older women, Cherokee women could share the task of child rearing. They often took children to the fields with them. Those old enough to help did so. Infants were bound to a cradleboard, a kind of portable crib, and mothers left them in the shade of a tree or perhaps even hanging from a low bough.

The Cherokees were very lenient with their children. Parents never spanked their offspring; the only physical punishment used was lightly

and cribs, similar to Selu's storehouse.

Unlike Selu, Cherokees could not rely on magic to fill their baskets with corn and beans, which they planted, tended, and harvested by hand. Each household had its own small garden but most food came from large fields that the villagers farmed communally. These fields lay in the fertile river valleys where corn grew well. The Cherokees planted their corn and beans together in hills: The bean vines ran up

The Cherokees lived in seasonal dwellings. In warm weather they needed only a wooden shelter (right), but when autumn arrived families settled into asi, *conical houses that featured a hearth in the center.*

scratching disobedient youngsters with thorns. The indulgence demonstrated by Selu, whose children even killed her, was perhaps excessive but demonstrated the tolerant spirit among Cherokees. Naughty children were often shamed into good behavior with teasing, which was supposed to humiliate them into mending their ways.

Women not only cared for children and farmed but also gathered firewood, carried water, and cooked food. Cherokees did not have regular meals and instead ate whenever they were hungry. Their favorite food was corn, which they prepared in many different ways. Most corn was allowed to ripen and dry in the fields. Then the hard kernels were soaked in water mixed with wood ashes (lye), a solution that removed the husk.

Women pounded the corn kernels in a mortar made from a tree trunk with a wooden pestle, which had a large end to give it weight. When they had finished pounding, they sifted the corn in order to separate the chunks from the fine meal. The chunks were used in soups and stews, which always stood near the doorway of Cherokee houses. The cornmeal was used for bread. Breads also included other ingredients, such as dried beans and chestnuts. Cherokees had no butter, but they used bear grease or the oil from pounded nuts on their bread.

The task of furnishing Cherokee houses fell to the women, who employed a variety of materials and techniques. They crafted benches for sleeping and sitting from saplings and made baskets, which had many uses, from river cane, strips of maple and oak, and honeysuckle. In order to decorate their baskets with unusual designs, women created dyes from bloodroot, butternut, walnut, and other plants. The Cherokees made some baskets with two layers of woven river cane; the double weaving made them particularly strong.

Pottery was made from native clay. The Cherokees had no potter's wheel so women coiled their pots from long ropes of clay. Then they smoothed the sides with a stone and stamped or cut a design into the outside. The unglazed pots were put in open fires to harden and thus acquired a dark black finish that reminded Europeans of cast iron.

Cherokee women also helped men dress deerskins and then fashioned the skins into clothes using needles made of bone. Sewing for the family was not too difficult because Cherokees normally wore very few clothes. In fact, children usually wore nothing at all. Women wore a short skirt, as did men. In winter they might add a skin cloak and moccasins that laced up to their knees. Women and children spent the cold months inside the winter house, where they were warm despite their scanty clothing. Both men and women were fond of jewelry and wore necklaces of shell, bone, and copper.

Men and women may have worn similar clothing, but they lived very separate lives. While women farmed, cared for children, cooked, made household goods, and did other domestic chores, men contributed to their family's livelihood by hunting. Like Kana'ti, men were responsible for providing their family with meat. The Cherokees kept no livestock before the arrival of Europeans, and so all meat was wild game—deer, bear, and turkey in particular. Winter was the season for hunting, and a hunting party would often be gone for several months in search of game. Cherokees hunted as far west as the Mississippi River and perhaps even beyond.

The most important game animal was the deer. The Cherokees ate the deer's flesh, tanned the animal's hide using a solution distilled from deer brains, wore the skins, made tools and ornaments from bones and antlers, and used sinews for thread and hooves for glue. They tried not to waste anything. The same was true with the bear and turkey. Cherokees prized bears for their thick fur and for their fat, which they rendered into grease. Bear claws doubled as jewelry. Turkeys provided not only meat but also feathers for personal adornment. The Cherokees used feather wands in ceremonial dances and fashioned capes from feathers by affixing them to a netting made of bark strips.

Cherokee men used bows and arrows to kill large game such as deer. They made points for their arrows by

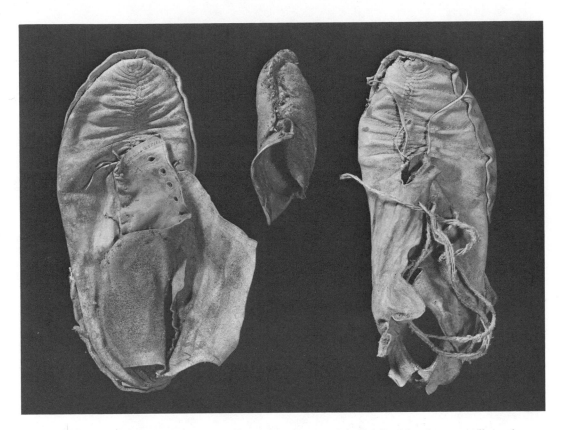

Cherokee women fashioned moccasins out of deerskin, sewing them with a bone needle and thread made from deer sinew.

chipping flint or other stones or by carving bone. Sometimes they used traps to capture bears. Birds and rabbits fell victim to smaller traps. Cherokees also used blowguns and darts to kill these animals. In fact, a boy had to demonstrate his mastery of the blowgun before he could advance to bow and arrow.

The Cherokees had several techniques for catching fish. They had hooks and nets as well as traps. Perhaps the most effective way of obtaining a fish dinner, however, was poisoning a stream. The Cherokees built a dam across the stream and then stirred an organic poison such as ground horse chestnuts into the water. The poison attacked the nervous system of the fish but caused no harm to the humans who later ate them. The paralyzed fish floated to the surface, and the fishermen simply selected the ones they wanted. When the dam was opened and fresh water diluted the poison, the other fish recovered and swam away.

When men were not hunting, they spent much of their time playing games that improved their coordination and kept them physically fit for the long winter hunts. They held arrow-shooting contests, hurled sticks at a rolling stone disk, and played stick ball. Stick ball, similar to modern lacrosse, was really much more than a mere game. Played by two teams with equal num-bers of participants, stick ball was called "the little brother to war." Players wielded one or two wooden rackets and hurled a hard deerskin ball up and down the field, trying to cross the opponent's goal line. Preparation for the game involved some of the same rituals as going to war, such as fasting and scratching the skin, and like warriors, stick-ball players often sustained seri-

Cherokees inserted darts such as these into their blowguns and often perfected their aim by practicing on round targets made of thistle. Hunters used blowguns to kill small game animals such as rabbits and birds.

ous injuries. Villagers had great enthusiasm for these games and often wagered on them.

When Europeans first witnessed these games, they failed to understand their importance. Furthermore, they did not believe that men were working when in fact they were. Early European visitors to the Cherokees compared the lives of men and women and decided that the men were lazy and that the women were as exploited as slaves. Europeans misunderstood the real role of women in Cherokee society. Women were by no means slaves; indeed, they had enormous power and authority. Part of their prominence came from the Cherokees' matrilineal kinship system.

In a matrilineal kinship system, people trace their descent through women instead of men or as we do in our culture, through both men and women. In Cherokee society, a person's only relatives were those on his mother's side. Relatives included a person's mother and the mother's mother, sisters, sisters' children, and brothers (but not her brothers' children). In other words, the Cherokees did not consider a child related by blood to the father or to the father's mother, sisters, and brothers.

A Cherokee belonged to his mother's clan, a group tracing its descent from a common ancestor. In the Cherokee kinship system there were seven clans, each of which bore a special name: Wolf, Deer, Bird, Paint, Long Hair, Blind Savannah, or Holly. (The translations of the last three are uncertain.) These clans were scattered throughout the Cherokee country. Every village probably had households representing each of the clans, and so a Cherokee could always find relatives in a village even if he had never been there before.

The Cherokees were matrilocal as well as matrilineal; that is, a family lived in the household of the mother. A man resided with his wife and children in a household that usually included her mother, her sisters, her sisters' children and husbands, and her unmarried brothers. If husband and wife divorced, as they did frequently in Cherokee society, the husband simply moved out of his wife's household and into the house of his mother and sisters. Children always stayed with their mother because, after all, they were not thought to be related to their father.

Children, of course, knew who their father was. They loved and respected him. The man who trained boys to hunt and decided when they were old enough to go to war, however, was not their father but their mother's brother, their uncle. He was the man to whom boys and girls owed their greatest respect. The mother's family, in other words, controlled the lives of children—another factor that probably contributed to women's prestige in Cherokee society.

As women held power within the family, so, too, they wielded influence within the village. In the village council, the traditional form of Cherokee government, prominent female members of the community freely voiced their opinions, as did well-respected men. Council meetings were run democratically; villagers debated an issue until they reached consensus. This model was repeated throughout the Cherokee homeland, in which individual settlements governed themselves—neither a chief nor a national council ruled the tribe as a whole until the 18th century. Government did not unify the Cherokees. Instead, a common language (although there were three or four dialects), the kinship system, and shared beliefs made the Cherokees one people.

One of the most serious questions a town council had to deliberate was whether or not to go to war. The Cherokees did not fight for territory or out of patriotism. The only reason they went to war was to avenge the deaths of Cherokees who had been killed by an enemy. The spirits of the dead could not go to the "darkening land," where they were supposed to dwell after death, until their kinsmen had taken revenge on their killers. The enemy could be other Native Americans—such as Creeks, Shawnees, Senecas, Chickasaws—or some other people. The council determined who was responsible for Cherokee fatalities and rallied support for a war party.

The size of war parties ranged from 2 or 3 to more than 100, but expeditions normally involved between 20 and 40 warriors. Clan members of those killed had a special obligation to avenge their relatives' death, and so they were the Cherokees most likely to join a war party. The decision to go to war was strictly up to an individual. If a warrior experienced uneasiness or suffered from nightmares about a particular expedition, he was thought to be receiving bad omens and was encouraged to remain at home. The Cherokees applauded anyone who had the good sense to pay attention to these signs.

The men who decided to participate in a raid assembled in the council house to prepare for battle. The Cherokees believed that victory would come only if warriors were spiritually pure, and so the men seeking vengeance fasted, drank black drink (a special tea containing lots of caffeine), took emetics in order to vomit and thus cleanse themselves, and participated in rituals designed to ensure victory. They followed this regimen for several days.

When the warriors left the village, they took great care to avoid detection and ambush. They traveled single file, and each warrior stepped into the footprint of the warrior in front of him. The warriors concealed their presence by imitating the natural sights and sounds of the forest. Sometimes they attached bear paws to their feet and followed the course bears might take in order to trick the enemy. They often communicated by whistling birdcalls or vocalizing other animal noises. The warriors wanted to take the enemy by surprise, quietly and quickly, and then withdraw. Sometimes pitched battles took place, but the Cherokees preferred the safety of ambush.

Because their objective was vengeance, the warriors hoped enemy casualties would equal the number of Cherokees who had been killed. Once they had taken the required lives, they went home. Eventually, the enemy would come for vengeance against the Cherokees, but for the time being, the war was over. For the Cherokees and their Indian neighbors, war was not a series of campaigns with a single goal, but rather a series of continuing raids. The Cherokees retaliated for an attack by the enemy, who then sought vengeance on the Cherokees, who once again retaliated. War was never ending.

Sometimes Cherokees captured some of the enemy. The fate of these

An 18th-century European woodcut depicts Cherokee fishermen in a canoe. The feathered headdress of the figure on shore depicts not Cherokee clothing but the European notion of "Indian dress."

captives rested with War Women. War Women accompanied many war parties to cook food and carry firewood and water, and some had distinguished themselves in battle. Nancy Ward was a War Woman of the Wolf clan who lived in the late 18th century. Later in life she married the trader Brian Ward and anglicized her name, but as a young woman, she was married to the warrior Kingfisher. She accompanied his war party, probably as cook and water carrier, on a raid against the Creeks. When Kingfisher was killed in battle, she seized his gun, rallied the Cherokees, and led her people to victory. The Cherokees honored her, as they had other women who demonstrated such bravery, with the title "War Woman," which gave her power over captives.

Although child and female captives were often adopted by Cherokee families, the War Women usually condemned warriors to the stake. Village women were in charge of the torture. Victims were beaten and burned, sometimes for several days, before they died. This practice seems horrifying today, but it made sense in terms of Cherokee beliefs. The Cherokees went to war for vengeance, but only men (and a very few women) participated in actual warfare. Torture gave all Cherokees an opportunity to help send the spirits of their dead to the darkening land.

Vengeance was also important to Cherokees because they believed that they must keep the world in balance, in a state of equilibrium. When a Cherokee died, the world was out of balance until the person responsible for that death also died. The Cherokees thought that if they did not maintain equilibrium, then droughts, storms, disease, or other disasters might occur. Cherokees believed that the principal people's major purpose was keeping the world in harmony and balance.

This view of their role in the world helps explain the Cherokee judicial system. The Cherokees had no policemen or law courts. If a person wronged another, it was up to the injured person or his clan to obtain retribution or vengeance. Murder, of course, was the most serious crime. If one Cherokee killed another, the world was out of kilter just as it would have been if the Cherokee had been killed by the enemy. In order to reestablish the balance, the murderer or one of his relatives had to die. Normally the murderer gave himself up, because he knew that if he did not, an innocent kinsman might suffer the penalty for his crime. The kinsmen of the murderer did not try to protect him, nor did they retaliate for his death. The death of the murderer restored harmony and balance.

The Cherokees' concern for harmony was evident in many areas of their life. Selu and Kana'ti, the providers of vegetables and meat, complemented each other. By hunting, men balanced women, who farmed. Summer, the season for farming, complemented winter, the season for hunting.

Thus Cherokees took care to do things in the appropriate season so as to preserve order.

Because the principal people sought to maintain harmony and balance in the world, they tried not to exploit nature. When a hunter killed a deer, for example, he performed a special ritual in which he apologized to the spirit of the deer and explained that his family needed food. Hunters never killed for sport. They believed that if they violated their sacred trust, terrible things would happen to them. The exploitation of animals could bring disease. If this happened, plants, which were a natural counterbalance to animals, could provide a cure.

Cherokee religion centered on sustaining harmony. At the Green Corn Ceremony the Cherokees tried to wipe out any disorder that had crept in during the year and begin anew. At this time, villagers cleaned private houses and the council house, threw away broken baskets and pottery, discarded any food left over from the preceding year, and extinguished old fires in a cere-monial gesture of renewal. The women presented the village with new corn, which had just become edible, and prepared a great feast. The Cherokees also dissolved unhappy marriages at this time and forgave all old wrongs except murder. People began the year with a clean slate and the knowledge that order had been restored.

Because the Cherokees killed game only when they needed it and destroyed any surplus at the Green Corn Ceremony, they never accumulated wealth. In fact, they strongly disapproved of anyone who tried to produce more than was needed to survive. This trait amazed early European visitors to the Cherokees, but it probably contributed to their generous hospitality, which Europeans also noted. The Cherokees had no real reason to impress each other or anyone else with worldly goods. They were, after all, the principal people, the descendants of Kana'ti and Selu. They lived in the center of the island that was the world, and they protected that world by maintaining harmony and order. ▲

During a visit to England in 1762 Cunne Shote (The Stalking Turkey), a prominent Cherokee chief and warrior, sat for this portrait by the English painter Francis Parsons.

CHEROKEES AND EUROPEANS

The principal people, living in the center of their island, were certainly no strangers to change. Their way of life had continuously evolved over thousands of years. Distant ancestors had survived by hunting big-game animals, long extinct; more recent ancestors had given up a nomadic existence for village life and farming. The development of agriculture had altered Cherokee society, and the rate of change accelerated with the introduction of corn, about 1,000 years before Europeans first encountered the Cherokees.

As significant as these innovations were, they probably were imperceptible to the Cherokees because they took place over such a long period of time. In contrast, the cultural changes that accompanied the arrival of Europeans were rapid, dramatic, and painfully obvious. Europeans threatened the Cherokees not only physically but also culturally and socially, forcing them to abandon their traditions.

The principal people first came into contact with Europeans in 1540. Hernando de Soto, a Spanish conquistador, passed through Cherokee territory on his exploration of what is today the southeastern United States. De Soto traveled with a large entourage of soldiers, horses, pigs, and native peoples whom he had enslaved to carry the expedition's supplies. He was looking for gold and silver or other forms of wealth that he could send home to Spain. In the Southeast, he was disappointed. He found no grand cities or rich mines such as those Spanish explorers had discovered in Mexico and Peru.

Instead, de Soto encountered farmers living in towns with populations ranging from hundreds to thousands. Even large communities, such as the fortified town he found in present-day Alabama, had no sumptuous palaces filled with riches. Subsequent Spanish expeditions such as that of Juan Pardo in the 1560s may have discovered small natural deposits of precious metals, but these early attempts to exploit the Indians and their resources were not very successful.

The explorations of de Soto, Pardo, and others did have an enormous impact on native peoples in the Southeast. Reluctant to accept the truth that the Indians had no gold, de Soto's soldiers tried to force natives to reveal the whereabouts of their nonexistent mines. Many people, unable to do so, died. Others became slaves of the Spaniards, and they acted as guides, translators, or bearers for the expedition. The Spanish justified their treatment of the Indians on the grounds that Native Americans were not Christians and, therefore, were not entitled to humane treatment.

As terrible as the physical abuse by the Spaniards must have been for the Cherokees and other native peoples, the most devastating effect of the Spanish expeditions came from an unseen and, at the time, unknown source—disease. Many of the diseases that afflicted Europeans did not exist in America. Because a vast ocean separated Europe and America, Indians had built up no natural immunities to European diseases. Among these were not only the great killers such as smallpox and bubonic plague, but also such diseases as measles, a virus from which most European sufferers quickly recovered. When an Indian contracted a European disease, however, his chances of survival were far less than those of an af-

flicted European. Measles, to say nothing of smallpox and plague, became a deadly disease for Native Americans.

The organisms that carried these diseases often spread ahead of European explorers. De Soto encountered villages that had been hit by epidemics shortly before his arrival. Some appeared to have been totally wiped out. Modern demographers, those who study population shifts, theorize that the first 200 years of the European presence in America brought about the demise of 95 percent of the native population, and disease was a major factor in this depopulation. This means that for every 100 Native Americans who lived in 1492, there were only 5 in 1692.

We know relatively little about the response of the Cherokees and other native peoples to the European invaders and their diseases. Surviving Cherokee oral tradition contains no mention of the conquistadors. We can speculate, however, how they might have regarded these people. The Cherokees, of course, knew that there were peoples other than the principal people living in the world. They had both traded with and sent war parties against Creeks, Choctaws, and Chickasaws to the south and Iroquois peoples to the north. These peoples were different from the principal people, and in one of their dances, the booger dance, the Cherokees made fun of what they saw as the peculiarities of these other Indians.

When Europeans arrived, the Cherokees incorporated them into the booger dance and depicted them as physically and sexually aggressive: The Indian playing the part of the European chased screaming girls around the dance ground. The Cherokees had no concept of race or of racial solidarity. They did not see other Native Americans as more closely related to them than Europeans. Europeans were simply different and particularly aggressive people.

Cherokees probably did not associate the new deadly diseases with Europeans. They believed that misfortune came about when the world was out of balance, and they turned to their priests to restore the balance. The priests, medicine men and women, presumably

De Soto's Discovery of the Mississippi *(circa 1868) by W. H. Powell. During his explorations in 1540, De Soto was the first European to make contact with the Cherokees.*

knew what plants to use and words to say to cure disease. Many of these new ailments, however, seemed to be beyond their power. They could not cure the European diseases or stop their progress. This must have produced doubts about the priests and their medicine. There is a Cherokee story about the people rising up and killing priests who had violated custom. We do not know whether the story is true or not, but it suggests that at some point, Cherokees began to question some of their traditional beliefs. The old remedies did not work for the new conditions with which the principal people were confronted.

Unlike native peoples along the coast, the Cherokees had some time to cope with the initial effects of European contact before the major onslaught began. After the conquistadors departed in the 16th century, the principal people had little contact with Europeans for about a hundred years. In the late 17th century, a few English traders from Virginia or Carolina probably traveled to their territory occasionally, but prolonged interaction did not come until the 18th century.

Traders were the first Europeans whom the Cherokees came to know well. Traders not only wanted to sell the Indians a variety of European manufactured goods, such as metal farming implements, but also wanted to buy deerskins, which were an important source of leather in Europe at this time. At first, traders came to the Cherokee country in late winter or early spring, when the men were returning with skins from the winter hunt. They exchanged the goods they had brought by packhorse from the English colonies for the skins, which they loaded on the horses for the return journey.

By the early 18th century, traders were beginning to build stores in the Cherokee country and to live there year round. Many of them married Cherokee women. A Cherokee wife helped make the trader a part of the Cherokee community. He could learn her native language from her or she could be his interpreter. Furthermore, his children by her were Cherokees: That is, in the Cherokees' matrilineal kinship system, the children of Cherokee mothers were Cherokees regardless of the race of the father.

Intermarriage with Cherokee women, however, upset traditional Cherokee social organization. The women came to live with their husbands, contrary to the Cherokee custom of husbands residing with their wives. Children took their father's name along with their mother's clan affiliation, and they inherited their father's houses, stores, and goods. These children introduced the first real inequality of wealth into Cherokee society. Furthermore, they often spoke English as well as Cherokee, received some education, and adopted many of the beliefs and customs of Europeans.

The traders who lived in the Cherokee country sent to Charleston, South

Carolina, or to some other port city for goods with which to barter. At the end of hunting season, they shipped the skins that Cherokee hunters sold them back to the coastal towns. By living in the Indian community, however, they could sell to their customers throughout the year, not just in the spring as the traveling traders had. These traders extended credit to hunters against the skins they would bring in the spring. In this way, many Indians became indebted to the traders.

Cherokees also gradually became dependent on the goods that the traders provided them, especially the metal tools such as hoes or knife blades, which the Cherokees found far superior to traditional stone ones. Two other commodities, guns and ammunition, quickly became necessities not only for hunting deer but for protecting the principal people from those enemies who were also armed. As the Cherokees used more and more of these European products, they abandoned their own crafts: People forgot how to chip a stone knife and lost much of their skill with the bow and arrow. Trade with Europeans became a necessity rather than a luxury.

At the same time, European demand for skins increased. Traders raised prices, and Indians had little choice but to provide more skins. In their renewed efforts to obtain more skins, hunters began to abandon their traditional attitude toward killing deer and their concern for keeping the world

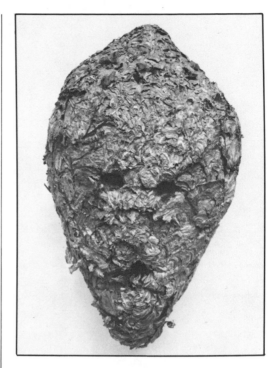

A booger mask constructed from a hornet's nest. Such masks caricatured enemies' features and were worn by the Cherokees in ritual booger dances to mock Europeans or hostile tribes.

in balance. The number of deer they slew increased dramatically. In 1708, for example, the Cherokees sold 50,000 skins to traders; by 1735 deerskin sales totaled 1,000,000.

In addition to deerskins, traders bought war captives from Cherokees. These captives were Indians of other tribes whom the Cherokees had captured. Originally, most of them would have been tortured or killed, but traders offered to buy them. Warriors relinquished their captives to traders, who

An engraving (circa 1863) depicts the port of Charleston, South Carolina. Earlier in the century, European traders used Charleston as a point of departure for their travels inland to meet with the Cherokees.

sent them to Charleston, where they were sold as slaves. These Indian slaves worked alongside African slaves on rice and tobacco plantations in America's mainland colonies or on sugar plantations in the West Indies. As Cherokees and other Indian peoples discovered the European market for captives, warfare increased and was motivated by the desire to take hostages rather than the wish to wreak vengeance.

Successful hunters and warriors achieved a new prominence in Cherokee society as the sole providers of European trade goods. Women who had previously enjoyed considerable freedom became dependent on men for such things as hoes, kettles, and even clothing (because skins were now sold). The new economic power of hunters and warriors brought an increased political power. Because others were dependent on them, their opinions in council began to carry more weight than those of people who did not have deerskins and captives to sell to the traders. This political power grew stronger when Europeans began to enlist Indian warriors to help fight their wars in North America.

The Cherokees became embroiled in the European struggle for North America in the 18th century. The Spanish held Florida; the French controlled Canada, the Mississippi valley, and Louisiana; the British occupied the Atlantic seaboard. Each wanted to dominate North America and sought Indian allies to help them. The Cherokees were never seriously tempted to aid the Spanish, who were too far away, but the British and French competed for Cherokee allegiance. Although the Cherokees usually sided with the British, many did transfer their allegiance to the French during the course of the Seven Years' War (1756–63).

At the beginning of this conflict—also called the French and Indian War—the Cherokees supported the English. Choctaw and Iroquois allies of the French repeatedly attacked Cherokee towns, and so the Cherokees asked the British to build forts and station soldiers in their territory to protect their homes and families. In 1756 the English built Fort Prince George in what is now South Carolina and Fort Loudoun in eastern Tennessee.

After the forts were completed, the Cherokees agreed to accompany the English on a campaign against the French and their Shawnee allies in the Ohio River valley. Heavy snows and swollen rivers cost the warriors their horses and provisions and forced them to turn back after six weeks. By the time they reached the Virginia frontier, the warriors desperately needed food. They happened on some cows that were grazing in the woods. The warriors regarded the unpenned livestock as game and appropriated it for food. When the English farmers who owned the livestock discovered their loss, they attacked the Cherokees, killed several, and took their scalps. Adding insult to injury, the Englishmen then claimed that the scalps belonged to enemy Indians and sold them to the Virginia legislature, which had offered a reward for such prizes.

When word of the attack reached Cherokee country, young warriors began to avenge the deaths of their kinsmen by raiding English settlements. Older headmen tried to restrain them and even sent a delegation to Charleston in 1758 to arrange a truce between the Cherokees and the British colonists. However, the raids continued. In November 1759, 32 of the most prominent Cherokee leaders assembled at Fort Prince George to work out an acceptable agreement with the South Carolina colonial governor.

The governor ignored the peaceful nature of their visit to the fort and imprisoned the entire party in a room intended for six soldiers. In exchange for the chiefs, the governor demanded the surrender of all Cherokees who had killed Englishmen and all Frenchmen who lived in Cherokee towns. A few concessions by the Cherokees prompted the governor to release the war chief Oconostota and two others. In February of 1760, Oconostota laid siege to Fort Prince George. After several weeks, he sent word that he wanted a conference with the fort's commander. When the lieutenant in charge stepped from the stockade, Oconostota signaled his warriors to attack. Immediately, the soldiers inside the fort burst into the room where they held the Cherokee hostages and massacred the 29 unarmed chiefs.

In retaliation, the Cherokees accelerated their attacks along the Carolina frontier and placed Fort Loudoun under siege. In June 1760, Colonel Archibald Montgomery and 1,600 soldiers invaded Cherokee territory. They destroyed all the "lower towns," located on the banks of the Savannah River, in what is now Georgia, slaughtered more than a hundred Cherokees, and drove the homeless survivors into the mountains. Montgomery then advanced toward the "middle towns," which rested on the banks of the Little Tennessee and Tuckaseigee rivers. On June 27 the Cherokees halted his progress near the present-day state line separating North and South Carolina. A large force of warriors ambushed the company, cut down nearly a hundred Englishmen, and forced Montgomery to retreat to Fort Prince George.

The defeat of Montgomery's force doomed Fort Loudoun. Cut off from help, the soldiers had to eat their dogs and horses. On August 8 the garrison surrendered. The Cherokees agreed to conduct their prisoners to the English settlements if they turned over all their guns and ammunition. The soldiers, however, buried most of their weapons or threw them in the river. This dishonesty sealed their fate: The next day at dawn, the Cherokees struck, killed 30 of the soldiers, and took the survivors captive.

The next summer, the English launched another expedition against the Cherokees. This time a force of 2,600 men including a number of Chickasaw and Choctaw warriors defeated the Cherokees. Following the example of Montgomery, the soldiers destroyed 15 middle towns. British lieutenant Francis Marion described a typical day of the campaign in his journal:

We proceeded, by Colonel [James] Grant's orders, to burn the Indian cabins. Some of the men seemed to enjoy this cruel work, laughing heartily at the flames, but to me it appeared a shocking sight. Poor creatures, thought I, we surely need not grudge you such miserable habitations. But when we came, according to orders, to cut down the fields of corn, I could scarcely refrain from tears. Who, without grief, could see the stately stalks with broad green leaves and tasseled shocks, the staff of life, sink under our swords with all their precious load. . . . I saw everywhere around the footsteps of the little Indian children, where they had lately played under the shade of their rustling corn. When we are gone, thought I, they will return, and peeping through the weeds with tearful eyes, will mark the ghastly ruin where they had so often played.

Famine resulted from the destruction of the corn crop and lowered the Cherokees' resistance to disease; a smallpox epidemic followed. According to some estimates, war, hunger, and disease reduced the Cherokee population to one-half its prewar total.

The Cherokees lost a considerable amount of territory after the war because Europeans required defeated Indian tribes to relinquish land. In 1770, a treaty deprived the Cherokees of their hunting grounds in Virginia and West Virginia. In 1772, the Cherokees surrendered the territory east of the Kentucky River, and in 1775, by a fraudulent land transaction, they "sold" their land to the west of that river. The loss of their primary hunting grounds following the Seven Years' War added to the economic distress the Cherokees suffered as a result of the ruin of their towns and fields.

The Cherokees lost the Seven Years' War, but they and other Indian peoples had inflicted serious casualties on the English colonies. Therefore, the British Crown attempted to appease native peoples and listened to their complaints, which centered around their resentment of colonists who illegally occupied Indian land. In order to remove this source of friction, the British tried to halt the westward movement of their colonists by prohibiting settlement beyond the Appalachian Mountains. Although some English violated this proclamation, the Indians recognized it as an attempt by the Crown to pre-

Austenaco, a Cherokee chief, led a hundred warriors against the Shawnee tribe in the French and Indian War.

vent mistreatment of native peoples.

This was one reason why most Cherokees sided with the British in the American Revolution. Encouraged by British agents and aided by Tories—colonists who took the side of the British Crown during the War of Independence—the Cherokees raided the frontiers of Georgia, Virginia, and the Carolinas in the summer of 1776. The rebellious colonists retaliated with a four-pronged invasion. The Cherokees, who still had not recovered from the Seven Years' War, were able to offer only minor resistance. The American soldiers remembered well how close the Cherokees had come to victory in 1760 and how frontier communities had suffered from raids. They intended to punish the Cherokees.

General Griffith Rutherford, who commanded the North Carolina troops, determined to demolish every one of the middle towns. The soldiers killed and scalped women as well as men, and they sold children into slavery. The Cherokees who escaped fled to the mountains where they lived exposed to the elements and subsisted on whatever wild foods they could find. All together, more than 50 towns were destroyed, most of them by Rutherford, and their residents were left without food or shelter.

The Cherokees recovered economically from the destruction of their towns, but suffered a long-lasting psychological trauma from the violence they had experienced. Twenty years after Rutherford's campaign, U. S. Indian agent Benjamin Hawkins discovered that when he rode into some Cherokee villages, the women were mute with fear. The children, who had heard of Rutherford's expedition from parents and grandparents, screamed in terror at the mere sight of a white man and hid until he left their village.

After the American Revolution, the majority of Cherokees favored peace and agreed to give up all lands east of the Appalachians. But a small band of warriors, called "Chickamaugas," were unwilling to accept a truce and moved their families to northeastern Alabama. With the assistance of the Spanish in Louisiana, they continued to fight until 1794. The Chickamaugas feared that the expansion of the United States spelled doom for the Cherokees and believed that by engaging in war they were protecting their territory the only way they could. The might of the United States, and particularly the Tennesseans, proved too great, however, and the Chickamaugas were forced to surrender after their towns were destroyed. Some chose to move west, but most decided to try to live in peace with white Americans.

The warfare of the 18th century brought change to the Cherokee political structure. Europeans did not want to deal with councils who deliberated at length over issues of war and peace. When Europeans wanted warriors to accompany their military campaigns, they did not want to partake in debates; they wanted the warriors *immediately*. Therefore, they gave gifts of guns, ammunition, textiles, tools, and other goods to prominent warriors who could provide them with manpower. Europeans recognized these men as chiefs, and they came to exercise unprecedented power in Cherokee society because they distributed the European goods to other warriors who were willing to go into battle, thus serving as the only link between the Cherokees and the whites. The responsibility for enforcing treaties and alliances fell to the war chiefs.

The warriors came to share political dominance with the descendants of traders. Traders and warriors were the people with whom all non-Indians interacted, and the most important political questions facing the Cherokees concerned non-Indians. For the Cherokees, this meant important changes. Instead of a council of all people making decisions for each town independently, a few individuals made and enforced decisions.

Most Cherokees did not object. They recognized that in their situation, they needed to delegate political power; someone had to be spokesman for the Cherokees, but they expected that person, or persons, to be responsible to them. Only if they had clearly designated officials could they prevent unauthorized sales of land. These officials also needed to enforce treaties and other laws in order to protect the people from retaliation for actions of a few. Individual Cherokees gave up some of their freedom and independence; they believed that in return, they had gained a degree of security for the principal people and their homeland. ▲

*Robert Lindneux's painting of Sequoyah shows the Cherokee leader
with the alphabet he invented. Around his neck hangs a medallion
presented to him by the administration of President James Monroe
during a trip to Washington, D.C.*

CHEROKEE "CIVILIZATION"

In the late 18th and early 19th centuries, the Cherokees faced a period of rebirth and regeneration—a renaissance. This renaissance grew out of desolation and desperation. At the end of the American Revolution, the Cherokees faced a severe economic depression. They had to relinquish to the United States large tracts of territory that included village sites as well as hunting grounds. The displaced people relocated, but many chose to live in isolated homesteads, less attractive to invaders, rather than in towns. The whole fabric of Cherokee society seemed to be disintegrating. The Cherokees, however, proved to be incredibly adaptable. They hoped that if they adopted the customs, beliefs, and lifeways of white Americans, they could survive as a people in their homeland.

The new U.S. government aided the Cherokees in this transformation because the leaders saw that it was to their advantage for the Cherokees to give up the hunting and warfare that had traditionally been central to Indian culture. Convincing Indians to abandon warfare was essential to the new nation's survival because the United States was very weak in its early years and could not afford an Indian war. Furthermore, some wanted the United States to expand, and they viewed the Indian hunting grounds as potential farms for white pioneers. If Indians gave up hunting, they would have no more use for hunting grounds. Therefore, they could be induced to sell this surplus land to the United States. In that way, the United States would obtain Indian land without a costly war.

Although some U.S. officials had ulterior motives, many of the individuals involved truly wanted to help the Indians. They saw the suffering of the Cherokees and other peoples and believed that only acceptance of the white man's way of life would save them from destruction. In order to "save" the Indians, the U.S. government developed a policy to "civilize" them. A "civilized" society, policymakers believed, was one composed of farmers who fenced their fields and used the plow as white men did. "Civilized" people were

Indian agent Return J. Meigs lived with the Cherokees for 22 years while he helped institute the government's "civilization" policy.

Christians who knew how to read and write the English language. They lived in houses like those of white men, ate meals at regular times, had proper table manners, dressed appropriately, and otherwise behaved like whites. "Civilized" people also governed themselves by written law, not custom, under a republican government like that of the United States. This very narrow view of human society had no appreciation for cultural differences between non-Indians and Native Americans.

The U.S. government sent agents to live with the Cherokees and other native peoples. The most successful agent to the Cherokees was Return J. Meigs, who lived among them from 1801 to 1823. Meigs established a farm modeled after those of white Americans and instructed the Cherokees in "civilized" life. He distributed plows to men and spinning wheels and looms to women. He hired blacksmiths and millers to set up shop in Cherokee country. Meigs and other agents also supervised trade between whites and Indians, and they sought to enforce laws against the sale of liquor, the consumption of which they regarded as harmful to Indian society.

Meigs, like other Indian agents, believed that the continuation of the deerskin trade with the Cherokees was detrimental to their "civilization" because it encouraged hunting rather than farming as a livelihood. For that reason, Meigs persuaded the Cherokees to cede their hunting grounds to the United States. In giving up this land, the Indians would by necessity give up hunting and would also clear the way for white pioneers. Thus Meigs aided white expansion into Cherokee territory and sometimes seemed to be working in the service of whites rather than of Indians.

The United States also encouraged and supported missionary work among the Cherokees. Agents and missionaries both believed that "civilization" and Christianity were inseparable: A person could not be a Christian without being "civilized," nor "civilized" without being Christian. The American government helped fund missions, and the missionaries instructed the Cherokees in farming and cooking as well as in the Bible.

Although there had been some missionaries among the Cherokees in the late 1700s, it was not until the next century that Protestant missionaries of German origin called "Moravians" established the first permanent mission outposts in the Cherokee homeland. In 1800 the Moravians obtained the consent of a Cherokee council to open a school. The Cherokees were not interested in Christianity, but they were anxious for their children to learn to read and write English. The Moravians built their mission school at Spring Place in present-day north Georgia. When they seemed more interested in converting than in teaching their students, the Cherokees threatened to banish them, and so they began their efforts at education in earnest. In fact, the Moravians found that most Cherokees were happy with their own religion: They won their first Cherokee convert to Christianity nine years after they had opened their mission.

The Moravians labored alone in the Cherokee nation until 1817, when the American Board of Commissioners for Foreign Missions opened a missionary station just south of present-day Chattanooga, Tennessee. The American Board was an interdenominational mission effort composed primarily of northern Presbyterians and Congregationalists and headquartered in Boston. The American Board was soon joined by both Baptists and Methodists.

The Methodists ministered to the Cherokees with traveling missionaries (also called circuit riders) who preached on the fly in open-air camp meetings and in Sabbath schools. Unlike the Moravians, they did not establish permanent outposts to perform their work among the Indians. Nor did they have boarding schools. Instead, children and adults were taught the rudiments of reading and writing on Sunday afternoons after services. The other denominations criticized the Methodists for this approach because they believed that the Indians needed intensive training and constant supervision to prevent them from lapsing back into their "savage" ways.

The majority of missionaries focused their efforts on the youngest members of Cherokee society. They thought that most adult Cherokees were too set in their ways to change dramatically. They had high hopes, however, for the children, particularly if they could be removed from the "harmful" influence of their parents and educated in boarding schools. The children who attended these boarding schools only occasionally visited their parents, and thus many of them gradually began to lose contact with their traditional culture. They accepted the missionaries' view of what was acceptable behavior and gradually came to regard their parents as "unenlightened."

In these boarding schools, the children learned the English language and studied arithmetic, geography, and other subjects. They read the Bible, prayed, and attended services regularly. The boys plowed, built fences, chopped wood, planted and harvested crops, and performed other tasks that missionaries thought were suitable for boys. Girls no longer worked in fields as their ancestors had; now they cooked, cleaned, ironed, sewed, and did other domestic chores deemed appropriate for young ladies.

Missionary societies, primarily in New England, supported children in mission schools by sending them clothing and books and contributing to the mission in the children's names. Children often wrote personal letters to their benefactors. Nancy Reece, a student at Brainerd, an American Board school, wrote a New England minister about her school in 1828:

> I will tell you something of our happy school, so you may know how we shall feel if we should be separated from each other, and from our teachers and other missionaries. Miss Ames has twenty-nine scholars; one more is expected which will make the school full. The studies in our school are Reading, Spelling, Writing, Geography, Arithmetick; two have begun to study grammar. Eight new scholars have entered school this year. Part of them cannot talk English, and Miss Ames is obliged to have me interpret for her. . . . When school hours are over, the girls attend to domestick concerns and learn to make their own clothes and the clothes of the boys so they can do

> such work when they go home, to assist their parents. They can then take care of their houses and their brothers and sisters and perhaps can learn their parents something that they do not understand. . . . The boys chop wood and in summer help about the farm and some that have left school are learning the black smiths trade.

Nancy Reece also wrote that she and her friends spent some of their spare time imitating New England missionary societies: They sewed bonnets and other items and then sold them to neighboring Cherokees. They sent the money to the American Board for the use of "the heathen who have not had missionaries as we have."

The children in mission schools did not always behave in ways that earned them the missionaries' approval. Cherokee children were very uninhibited: Boys and girls swam together without clothing and played games together wearing little more. They talked openly about sex and made off-color jokes to each other. Missionaries also found them vain and complained that they loved the pretty clothes and ornaments that the teachers thought were frivolous. The missionaries, however, had to use care in punishing children. Cherokee parents rarely disciplined their children and never used corporal punishment. If they discovered that a missionary had spanked a child, they often withdrew the child from school. Therefore the missionaries resorted to another form of punishment: They required students to memorize Bible verses appropriate to their infractions.

Missionaries and agents were remarkably successful in transforming the Cherokees' culture but only because many Cherokees had decided that these changes were in their own best interest. Parents sent their children to school, even with the understanding that they might become estranged from them, because they wanted their children to be able to deal more effectively with whites. In time, many adult Cherokees adopted the values of mainstream American culture themselves. For example, men now worked in the fields instead of women and came to believe that a woman's proper place was in the home.

The Cherokee nation officially adopted the "civilization" program of the U.S. government because Cherokee leaders believed that if their people were culturally indistinguishable from whites, the white people would permit them to live in peace in their homeland. The Cherokee government supported the work of the missionaries and sought to further the educational opportunities of its citizens. With the help of missionaries, the nation managed to buy a printing press and typefaces in both English and in the alphabet invented by the Cherokee Sequoyah.

Sequoyah had been born about 1770. Although his father may have been white, he had a traditional Cherokee childhood and never learned English. He did recognize, however, the

The letters of the Cherokee alphabet, as invented by Sequoyah. The Sequoyahan syllabary brought written communication to the Cherokees.

tremendous advantage English speakers enjoyed by being able to write their language. He wanted his own people to have that advantage. About 1809 he began to work on a Cherokee alphabet. Sequoyah struggled for about a decade. Finally he arrived at a system that worked, and within months he had developed 86 symbols (later reduced to 85) that stood for Cherokee syllables.

Because Sequoyah knew no alphabet, he invented his own symbols for

Cherokee. Some of his "letters" resemble those from the alphabet in which English is written; some appear to be adapted from the Greek alphabet, which Sequoyah may have seen at a mission station; others seem to have been created by him. Whatever their origins, the symbols of the Sequoyah alphabet, called a "syllabary," provided an efficient way to write the Cherokee language. The Cherokees enthusiastically adopted Sequoyah's syllabary and soon used it in place of a rival writing system developed by white missionaries. The system was remarkably easy to learn: Anyone who spoke Cherokee fluently could reportedly read and write the language in a few days. The Cherokees quickly became a literate people.

In 1828, the *Cherokee Phoenix*, a bilingual newspaper, began publication under the editorship of Elias Boudinot, a young Cherokee man who had been educated in mission schools in the Cherokee nation and in New England. In columns of alternating Cherokee and English, Boudinot printed the laws of the nation, local news, world news,

The front page of the July 9, 1828, edition of the Cherokee Phoenix. *This bilingual newspaper contained columns in both English and Cherokee.*

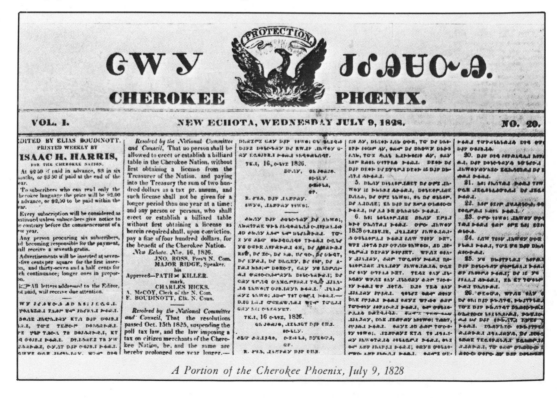

A Portion of the Cherokee Phoenix, July 9, 1828

human interest stories, Bible passages, editorials, and advertisements. Subscribers to the paper included not only Cherokees but interested whites in the United States and Europe.

The *Cherokee Phoenix*, the Sequoyan syllabary, and the mission schools all owed their existence to the civilization program of the U.S. government. Another outgrowth of the program was the development of commercial agriculture among the Cherokee. Because they held the title (or legal ownership) to their country in common, the Cherokees did not need to buy land, and therefore could farm as much land as they wished as long as they did not infringe on acreage that had already been claimed. The Cherokees who accumulated money through business ventures other than farming could invest their earnings in improvements on their property. Most prosperous Cherokees bought African slaves to work their fields and expanded their farms into plantations. They built elegant houses, which they embellished with imported furniture, china, and other luxury items. Some prosperous Cherokees added to their wealth by operating stores, mills, ferries, taverns, and toll roads. These men were wealthy by anyone's standards.

Among these Cherokee planters were the brothers John and Lewis Ross. Descendants of traders and Cherokee women, the Rosses owned several stores and plantations. John Ross, who was principal chief of the Cherokees from 1827 until his death in 1866, lived in a 2-story weatherboard house with 4 fireplaces and 20 glass windows, sumptuous fixtures for the time.

Ross's plantation at the head of the Coosa River in present-day north Georgia included workshops, smokehouses, stables, corn cribs, a blacksmith shop, a wagon house, and slave quarters. By 1835, Ross owned 19 slaves. He grew corn, wheat, and cotton and had peach and apple orchards. He also operated a ferry on the Coosa River and made a profit of about $1,000 per year.

John's brother Lewis owned several stores, a mill, 3 ferry boats, and more than 40 slaves. He lived in what visiting New Englanders described as "an elegant white house near the bank of the river, as neatly furnished as almost any in Litchfield County [with] Negroes enough to wait on us." Perhaps the wealthiest man in the Cherokee nation was John Ross's friend Joseph Vann, who lived in a magnificent redbrick mansion at Spring Place in north Georgia. In 1835 he owned 110 slaves who cultivated 300 acres, and he operated a mill, ferry, and tavern.

The accumulation of individual property led many Cherokees to believe that they needed a more formal legal system in order to protect their holdings. In 1808 a council of delegates from the major towns met, and in the first written Cherokee law, they established a national police force, called the Lighthorse Guard, to protect property. The system overrode many Cherokee tra-

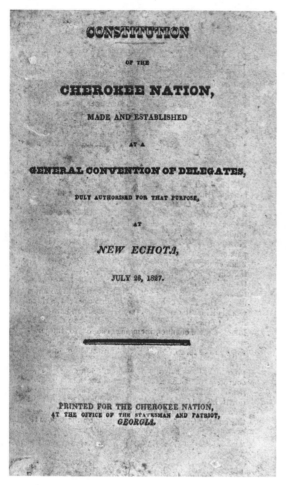

CONSTITUTION

OF THE

CHEROKEE NATION,

MADE AND ESTABLISHED

AT A

GENERAL CONVENTION OF DELEGATES,

DULY AUTHORISED FOR THAT PURPOSE,

AT

NEW ECHOTA,

JULY 26, 1827.

PRINTED FOR THE CHEROKEE NATION,
AT THE OFFICE OF THE STATESMAN AND PATRIOT,
GEORGIA.

The title page of the Cherokee Constitution, written in 1827 and modeled on the United States Constitution.

ditions. For example, it guaranteed that the wife would inherit her husband's possessions after he died, whereas Cherokee custom had dictated that a man would leave his property to his sister and her children.

As the Cherokee formalized their judicial code, so, too, they reorganized their method of governing. Cherokee councils were no longer acting independently and instead joined together to create a true national government—a ruling body that rendered the traditional town councils obsolete. Although they might still resolve local disputes, councils no longer wielded the power they once had. Most Cherokees, even those who were not wealthy, supported this change. They believed that a strong central government would be best able to protect the land that all Cherokees held in common. A central government that could be held accountable to Cherokee voters would be less likely to succumb to pressure and bribes from whites who were trying to obtain Cherokee land. In 1817 the Cherokees divided their nation into eight electoral districts, each of which sent representatives to the national council.

The Cherokees not only empowered their national government to protect personal and common property, but also gave the government judicial power—the right to determine guilt and innocence in criminal cases. The fate of criminals had previously been determined by clans within each of the villages, but in 1810 representatives of the seven clans renounced blood vengeance, thus surrendering judicial power to the emerging national government. District courts eventually tried criminal cases, and in 1822 the Cherokees established a supreme court to hear appeals from the district courts.

The culmination of this trend toward centralization and formalization of political power came in 1827 when the Cherokees wrote a constitution modeled after that of the United States:

WE, THE REPRESENTATIVES of the people of the CHEROKEE NATION in Convention assembled, in order to establish justice, ensure tranquility, promote the common welfare, and secure to ourselves and our posterity the blessing of liberty: acknowledging with humility and gratitude the goodness of the sovereign Ruler of the Universe, in offering us an opportunity so favorable to the design, and imploring his aid and direction in its accomplishment, do ordain and establish this Constitution for the Government of the Cherokee Nation.

The constitution provided for the General Council, a legislature composed of 2 houses: the National Council, a body of 32 members, and the 13-member National Committee. The Cherokees directly elected members of both houses. The General Council, in turn, chose the executive branch of the government, which consisted of the principal chief, the vice-principal chief, and the treasurer of the Cherokee nation. The judicial branch, established by earlier legislation, continued to assume responsibility for weighing guilt and meting out punishments for crimes. Neither women nor the descendants of African slaves could vote under this document. Unlike the Constitution of the United States, the Cherokee constitution defined the geographical boundaries of the Cherokee nation. In this way, the Cherokees indicated that they had no intention of expanding and, more important, that they intended to remain in their homeland. The constitution also affirmed that Cherokee land belonged to the nation and not to individuals. An individual, therefore, could not simply sell his land and move west. Only the nation could sell land, and this it would not do.

The writing of a republican constitution, the establishment of mission schools, the development of commercial agriculture, and the invention and adoption of Sequoyah's syllabary reflect profound changes that forever altered the fabric of Cherokee life. This transformation should not be interpreted simply as the destruction of traditional Cherokee society. Even in the face of intense pressure from whites, Cherokees maintained some control over the evolution of their culture. Although schools, churches, constitutions, and syllabaries were adopted from Anglo-Americans, the Cherokees used them to serve their own purposes. In some respects, the "civilization" of the Cherokees was really cultural revitalization that produced an intense pride in being Cherokee and a sense of Cherokee nationalism previously unknown in the history of the principal people. ▲

George Lowrey, a prominent Cherokee of mixed-blood ancestry, was a delegate to the 1827 constitutional convention and assumed the office of assistant principal chief in 1829.

REMOVAL

The creation of the Cherokee republic in 1827 precipitated a crisis for the U.S. government. The territory that the constitution explicitly delineated as belonging to the Cherokee nation was identical to that already occupied by four states—Georgia, Alabama, Tennessee, and North Carolina. The United States claimed that a Cherokee republic was illegal because it violated state sovereignty, as set forth by the U.S. Constitution in Article IV, Section 3: ". . . . no new State shall be formed or erected within the jurisdiction of any other State . . ." In formally asserting their right to their tribal lands, the Cherokees had created a state within a state, a violation of federal U.S. law. Thus, they gave the state governments an opportunity to challenge the Indians' right to the land and to promote the removal of all Indians to territory west of the Mississippi River, thereby opening the Indian land to white settlers.

Relations between Cherokees and the U.S. government had long suffered from disputes over land, despite decades of treaties and negotiations. The states' claim to Cherokee land rested on the precedent established by Europeans when they first arrived in the Americas in the 16th century. In fact, the American attitude toward the principal people can be traced directly to the views of the earliest European explorers to the New World, who had posed the question, "Who owns the land?" Because they wanted the land and all the riches it promised, Europeans were reluctant to admit that Native Americans had legitimate claim to the territory that they had occupied for centuries. The Indians had no absolute right of ownership, Europeans insisted, because they were not Christians and because they had not put the land to its "proper use." Therefore, the European nations argued, the Indians had only the right to *use* the land, but its ultimate ownership rested with the foreign countries that had discovered it.

During the 17th century, English colonists in North America agreed to purchase land rights from Native Americans if the latter agreed to vacate their territory. The treaties governing these deals usually called for the Cherokees and neighboring tribes to turn over valuable holdings for a pittance. Tribal leaders signed away thousands of acres to the British without understanding that they were, in effect, being robbed of their land.

After the American Revolution, the United States inherited English claims to the very same territory and also adopted British methods of negotiating with the Indians. The new Republic forced the Cherokees into a series of punitive treaties—retaliation for the Indians' alliance with the British during the War of Independence—that ceded large portions of the Cherokee homeland to the U.S. government. No sooner had they claimed this new turf than the Americans set their sights on an even greater share of Indian land, but they knew they must win it without a costly war.

The "civilization" program was an indirect means of obtaining Cherokee holdings because it moved the tribe— in the words of one historian—"out of the forest and onto the farm." Whites hoped that Cherokee farmers would relinquish their claim to the tribe's hunting grounds, which would then fall into the hands of the U.S. government. But the civilization program served another purpose, too. In the early years of the United States, many people believed that if Indians did not adopt the ways of whites and become assimilated into Anglo-American society, they would die out. Thus, they argued that the pro-

gram would save the Indians from certain extinction.

Many Indians, even among the Cherokees—most of whom enthusiastically participated in the government's efforts to "civilize" them—rejected aspects of the government's program. A majority of the opponents lived in small isolated villages and continued to conduct their lives in accordance with Cherokee tradition. They preferred town councils to a centralized republican government, found the lessons taught by elders and family far superior to those offered by mission schools, and rejected the teachings of Christianity.

In the late 18th century, many Cherokees who opposed peaceful relations with the United States moved west into present-day Texas and Arkansas. Other Cherokees who wanted to continue a lifeway based on hunting joined them. Cherokees from the East sometimes visited their western brothers to hunt game, which had become scarce in the East, or to make war on the Osage, their traditional enemies.

But those Cherokee traditionalists who remained in the East began to actively oppose assimilation within the Cherokee nation during the 1820s: They objected to the presence of missionaries and threatened rebellion when the Cherokee council called the Constitutional Convention in 1827. The persistence of traditional culture troubled acculturated leaders such as Principal Chief John Ross and *Cherokee Phoenix* editor Elias Boudinot. Missionaries and U.S. agents also found this traditionalism disturbing.

The resistance of some Cherokees to the "civilization" program seemed to confirm what many Americans were beginning to believe about Indians—that they were primitive peoples whose behavior would always be dictated by their inferior racial traits. Whites unjustly charged that most Cherokees were still "savages" and that Cherokee leaders concealed this "savagery" in order to protect their own power and property. These whites demanded that the Cherokees and other Indians be removed from "civilized" society.

Where then were the Cherokees to go? President Thomas Jefferson provided an answer: "Uncivilized" Indians could go to a new U.S. territory (now the state of Louisiana) that had been acquired by the United States in 1803 as a part of the Louisiana Purchase. This territory extended from the Mississippi River to the Rocky Mountains and from the Gulf of Mexico to what is today Canada. The land in the Louisiana territory included what are today the states of Arkansas, Kansas, Louisiana, Nebraska, Oklahoma, and parts of Iowa, Minnesota, Missouri, and South Dakota. The purchase of this vast area doubled the land mass of the United States.

Jefferson suggested that the eastern Indians could move to this wilderness and perhaps adopt "civilization" at their own pace. He ignored the other Indian nations who already claimed this

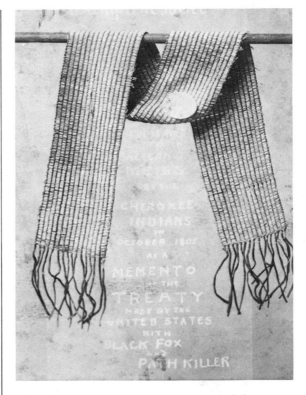

The Cherokees presented this wampum belt to Agent Meigs as a token of the agreement signed between the federal government and the Cherokee leaders Black Fox and Path Killer. The treaty called for the Indians to cede eastern lands in exchange for western territory.

territory as their homeland. After Congress had confirmed the Louisiana Purchase, it had also authorized the president to negotiate exchanges of land and the removal of eastern Indians to the West. Exchanges were, of course, supposed to be entirely voluntary.

Jefferson's efforts to convince eastern Indians to move west created a crisis for the Cherokees in 1808. At this time the Cherokees were not yet a centralized nation. Although a national council composed of representatives from traditional towns met annually and a principal chief spoke for the Cherokee nation, serious disagreements existed between two regions. The lower towns in Alabama and Georgia were much more committed to "civilization" and to assimilation than the upper towns of western North Carolina and eastern Tennessee.

Leaders of the lower towns favored an exchange of territory and persuaded Principal Chief Black Fox to support them. The opponents of the removal deposed Black Fox and made one of their number, Path Killer, principal chief. The actions of lower town chiefs did not reflect the wishes of the Cherokees in their region who, like a majority of Cherokees across the homeland, opposed removal to the West. The U.S. government knew that most Cherokees wanted to prevent the exchange of eastern for western land, but they persisted in their efforts to relocate the Indians. Unable to obtain a treaty from the national council, U.S. commissioners finally got an agreement from lower town chiefs. These leaders signed a treaty and then departed for their new homes in what is now Arkansas, accompanied by their followers.

Another major Cherokee land cession and emigration took place in 1817–19. Once again, U.S. treaty commissioners negotiated with minority chiefs and virtually bribed them into signing a treaty. For those who elected to go west under the treaties of 1817 and 1819, the U.S. government agreed to pay wealthy Cherokees the full value of their improvements, that is, their houses, barns, fences, and orchards. Poor Indians were promised "a rifle, ammunition, blanket, and brass kettle or beaver trap each, as full compensation." The United States also pledged to pay the cost of their removal to the West.

The new agreement mirrored the 1810 treaty in its promise of land "exchange," but differed from it in a unique clause known as the "reservation clause." U.S. commissioners offered Cherokees who lived within the ceded territory an opportunity to remain on their land. Anyone who chose to become a U.S. citizen could receive a reservation of 640 acres. A "reservation" was a privately owned tract of land within ceded territory. An Indian receiving such a reservation could do whatever he wished with it within the limits of U.S. law: He could sell it, lease it, or live on it.

About 150 Cherokees took advantage of this provision. Some wanted the land for speculation; that is, they planned to hold it until land values went up and then sell it for a profit. Other Cherokees, however, wanted to live on their reservations and become U.S. citizens, but a number of problems arose that forced most of these people to return to the Cherokee nation. Some had reservations located on land which had already been granted to veterans of the War of 1812 by the United States. Others had reservations occupied by squatters, who refused to move. Finally, increasingly harsh racial attitudes and state laws discriminated against Indians as "people of color." Holders of reservations preferred equality in the Cherokee nation to second-class status in the United States.

The land exchanges of both 1810 and 1817–19 held surprising consequences for both Jefferson and later proponents of removal. They had hoped that Cherokee traditionalists, people who wanted to preserve the old way of life, would go west while progressives, people who had adopted Anglo-American culture, would become assimilated. A few Cherokees who moved west were indeed traditionalists, but a surprisingly large number were progressives. Some progressives went west to escape political enemies who held treaty signers responsible for the loss of land in the East. Some no doubt sought to distance themselves from the increasingly racist Anglo-American society that refused to acknowledge their accomplishments. Still others, like many white pioneers, may have gone west in search of greater economic opportunities.

A sketch by George Catlin, an artist who traveled among various Indian tribes in the early 19th century, of the Cherokees before removal to Oklahoma.

Most Cherokee traditionalists, however, refused to move west. Many progressives did not understand the profound attachment these Cherokees felt to the land. The Cherokees, traditionalists believed, lived in the center of the world. Why should they move to the edge of the "island"? Traditionalists had a long list of objections to moving west: They believed that the spirits of the dead lived there; they viewed the mountains and valleys of their homeland as a holy place; they feared that the native plants from which they made sacred medicines used to cure physical and spiritual ills did not grow in the West.

Another unforeseen consequence of these early removals was the waning enthusiasm for westward migration among those Cherokees who remained in the East. U.S. government officials had hoped that the trickle of emigrants would swell to a stream. Instead, those Indians who wanted to go west simply went, thereby relieving eastern Cherokees of a proremoval faction. These removals also deprived U.S. negotiators of individuals who might be inclined to sign another removal treaty.

Opposition to removal, in fact, increased among Cherokees remaining in the East. One reason the Cherokees formalized their political system, recorded their laws, and wrote their constitution was to protect their homeland. The National Council served notice to the United States in 1819 that the Cherokees would cede no more land. They

Andrew Jackson, elected president of the United States in 1828, had earned fame as an "Indian fighter" in the U.S. Army and supported the removal of the Cherokees.

also soon enacted a law that reaffirmed and committed to writing an earlier understanding that any Cherokee who signed a treaty selling land would be executed.

Cherokee resolve to remain in the East strengthened at the very time that white southerners became more determined that the Indians should go west. Cotton quickly was becoming king in the South, and the Indians occupied land suitable for cotton growing. Southern states demanded that the federal government, which controlled Indian relations, expel the Indians. Georgia, the cotton state with the largest Cherokee population, insisted that the federal government live up to the terms of the Compact of 1802.

In this agreement, the state gave up territory, which eventually became Alabama and Mississippi, on the condition that the federal government extinguish Indian title to land within the state. Most people believed that this could be done easily through treaties, and until 1819, the federal government had been making some progress with the Cherokees. But their refusal to make any further cessions meant that the federal government could not fulfill the Compact of 1802. Georgians were furious. The discovery of gold at about the same time in the Cherokee country no doubt contributed to the Georgians' indignation.

The Cherokees' establishment of a republican government with a written constitution in 1827 gave Georgia an opportunity to press their claim to Cherokee land by accusing the principal people of violating state sovereignty. In order to reaffirm state power over territory within the Cherokee nation, the Georgia legislature abolished the Cherokee government and prohibited the council from meeting. The state legislature extended Georgia law to include the Cherokees, passed a series of discriminatory acts that forbade the Cherokees from mining their own gold, from using their own court system, and from testifying against whites in Georgia courts. The state then created a special police force, the Georgia Guard, to enforce these laws among the Cherokees. The legislature clearly wanted to make life so miserable for the Cherokees that they would leave. The legislators also authorized a survey and distribution of Cherokee lands to whites in a lottery.

During this time the Cherokees received little help from the federal government, least of all from the executive office, occupied by President Andrew Jackson from 1828 to 1837. Jackson had achieved fame as an Indian fighter, and he had negotiated several questionable treaties with the Cherokees and neighboring Indians. The president was determined to acquire Cherokee land and open it to white settlement. He offered the Cherokees a choice: They could accept the discriminatory laws of the states or they could move west. He, of course, believed that they should move. In 1830 Congress passed the Indian Removal Act, which authorized the president to negotiate with the Indians and appropriated $500,000 for that purpose. The Cherokees, fearing that the appropriation would be used for bribes, were distressed by the congressional action, but they also were determined to resist.

The suffering experienced by the Creeks, Choctaws, and Chickasaws, other Indians who did negotiate removal treaties, strengthened the Cherokees' resolve to remain in their homeland. They turned to the U.S. courts for justice. In 1831 the United

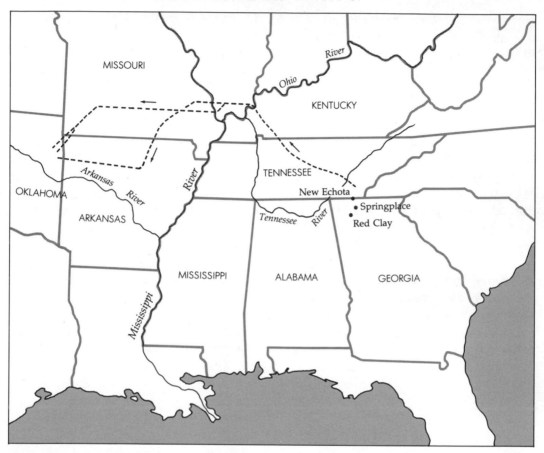

THE ROUTES TAKEN BY THE CHEROKEE DURING THEIR
REMOVAL TO THE WEST IN 1838–39

States Supreme Court ruled in *Cherokee Nation v. Georgia* that the Cherokee nation was a "domestic dependent nation" and had no standing before the court. Refusing to give up, the Cherokees hoped for a more conclusive and beneficial ruling the next year in *Worcester v. Georgia*.

Samuel A. Worcester was a white missionary to the Cherokees. The Georgia Guard arrested him and another missionary for violating the state law that required all whites living in the Cherokee nation to take an oath of allegiance to the state. Because Worcester was a citizen of the United States, he clearly had standing before U.S. courts of law. In this case, the Cherokees triumphed. The Court ruled that Georgia law did not extend over the Cherokees and ordered the state to release the missionaries. The Cherokee victory, however, was short lived. The Georgia government ignored the ruling of the Supreme Court. Legal technicalities coupled with an unwillingness to help the Cherokees kept Jackson from enforcing the decision. The missionaries remained in prison, and Georgians continued to harass the Cherokees.

When it became obvious that the Supreme Court decision would have little impact on the situation in the Cherokee nation, a small group of Cherokees began to consider negotiating removal. Known as the Treaty party, this group's leaders included Major Ridge—who had fought with the United States in the War of 1812—his college-educated son John, and his nephew Elias Boudinot,

who had edited the *Cherokee Phoenix*. Motivated at least as much by economic and political ambitions as by concern for the Cherokee people, the Treaty party enjoyed little support within the Cherokee nation.

The vast majority of Cherokees supported Principal Chief John Ross in his steadfast opposition to removal. Nevertheless, U.S. treaty commissioners met with about 100 Treaty party members in December 1835, and they negotiated the Treaty of New Echota. This treaty provided for the exchange of all Cher-

The Trail of Tears (1840) by Robert Lindneux. On their journey west, between one-fourth and one-half of the Cherokees died of exhaustion, exposure, and disease.

THE TRAIL OF TEARS, AS SEEN THROUGH THE EYES OF A WHITE MAN

John G. Burnett was a U. S. Army private during the winter of 1838–39. A native of Tennessee, he spent many days in his youth hunting in the hills and forests of the Cherokee nation and came to know them well. He felt a deep attachment to the Cherokee, despite his eventual induction into the army and his participation in the removal of the Cherokee from their homeland. In 1890, nearly 50 years after the Cherokee had trekked from Georgia to Oklahoma, Burnett recorded his account of the Trail of Tears.

The removal of the Cherokee Indians from their life long homes in the year of 1838 found me a young man in the prime of life and a Private . . . in the American Army. Being acquainted with many of the Indians and able to fluently speak their language, I was sent as interpreter into the Smokey Mountain Country [where I] witnessed the execution of the most brutal order in the history of American warfare. I saw the helpless Cherokees arrested and dragged from their homes, and driven at the bayonet point into the stockades. And in the chill of a drizzling rain on an October morning I saw them loaded like cattle or sheep into six hundred and forty-five wagons and headed for the West. . . .

The trail of the exiles was a trail of death. They had to sleep in the wagons and on the ground without fire. I have known as many as 22 of them to die in one night of pneumonia due to ill treatment, cold and exposure. Among this number was the beautiful Christian wife of Chief John Ross. This noble hearted woman died a martyr to childhood, giving her only blanket for the protection of a sick child. She rode thinly clad through a blinding sleet and snow storm, developed pneumonia and died in the still hours of a bleak winter night. . . .

The long painful journey to the west ended March 26, 1839, with four thousand silent graves reaching from the foothills of the Smokey Mountains to what is known as the Indian Territory in the West. And the covetousness on the part of the white race was the cause of all that the Cherokees had to suffer.

---

okee territory in the Southeast for a tract of land in what is today northeastern Oklahoma.

Fifteen thousand Cherokees, almost the entire population, signed a petition protesting this treaty, which had been signed by an unauthorized minority. Nevertheless, the U.S. Senate ratified the document. The treaty gave the Cherokees two years to go west. Confident that justice would ultimately triumph, the Cherokees made no preparations to move. Finally, in the summer of 1838, federal troops entered the Cherokee nation and began rounding up the Cherokees and imprisoning them in stockades. The soldiers often burned the captives' cabins and crops in order to discourage them from escaping and returning home. In the soldiers' sweep of Indian villages, parents and children often became separated.

Once they reached the stockades, the Cherokees did not have enough food or water. Chief Ross and other Cherokee leaders appealed to President Martin Van Buren, Jackson's successor in the White House, to permit the Cherokees to conduct their own removal to the West. Van Buren consented, and in the winter of 1838–39 the Cherokee nation moved west. This forced migration came to be known as the Trail of Tears because of the Cherokees' suffering. Between one-fourth and one-half of them died before reaching their new home in the West.

Cherokee removal ranks as one of the greatest tragedies in American history. The Cherokees, more than any other native people, tried to comply with the United States "civilization" program. They had become literate, Christian farmers governed by republican laws. Yet in the end none of that mattered as much as the whites' desire to clear the southeastern United States of Cherokees in order to make way for the territorial expansion of the United States. ▲

Elias Cornelius Boudinot, Jr., the son of Elias Boudinot, supported his father and Stand Watie in their defiance of Chief John Ross, who did not support removal to the West.

THE CHEROKEES IN THE WEST

In the spring of 1839 the Cherokees who survived the Trail of Tears joined two other branches of the principal people in the West: the Treaty party and the Old Settlers. Most members of the Treaty party, fearing reprisals from their countrymen, had left the Cherokee nation in the East promptly after signing the Treaty of New Echota in 1835. They traveled to what is today northeastern Oklahoma, where the western Cherokees, known as the Old Settlers, lived. In the first decade of the 19th century, the Old Settlers moved from the East to Arkansas, which, like Oklahoma, was part of Jefferson's Louisiana Purchase. They had intended to settle there permanently, but within 20 years white frontiersmen demanded their removal. In 1828 they moved further west, taking their customs and institutions with them.

The Old Settlers, the Treaty party, and the National party—as those who opposed removal were known—now occupied the same territory, but the differences among them produced considerable conflict in the new Cherokee nation in the West. For example, Old Settler Cherokees resented the newcomers, particularly the National party, who greatly outnumbered them. The Old Settlers were understandably apprehensive about the influx of thousands of Cherokees because the former had their own laws and chiefs, and they did not want to come under the rule of the far more numerous newcomers.

A more severe conflict divided the members of the Treaty party and the National party. These groups bore great enmity for one another because in the East they had clashed over the issue of removal. Because they went west before their eastern adversaries, members of the Treaty party had an opportunity to forge an alliance with the Old Settlers prior to the arrival of Chief John Ross and the majority of Cherokees. The Old Settlers found allies among the Treaty party, whose members certainly did not want to become subject to the rule of people who regarded them as traitors. Therefore, when the main body of Cherokees from the East arrived they found an alliance of the Treaty party and Old Settlers that opposed the instatement of the eastern Cherokee nation's institutions, laws, and leaders in the West—which was exactly the course of action that Principal Chief John Ross and his followers had in mind.

In order to iron out their differences, the National party and the Old Settlers formally met in June 1839, but they reached no new accord. The Old Settlers could not understand why the eastern Cherokees refused to accept the government they found in the West, as had the members of the Treaty party. Plans were made for another meeting of the Old Settlers and the eastern Cherokees, and there was hope that the two groups could resolve their problems.

Before the second meeting could take place, chaos erupted among the Cherokees. At dawn on June 22, a group of armed men dragged John Ridge from his bed and into the yard where they stabbed him to death as his family looked on in horror. Later in the morning, his father, Major Ridge, was shot from his horse. At about the same time, several men asked Elias Boudinot for medicine that he normally dispensed from a nearby mission. On the way to the mission, they stabbed him repeatedly. Others, too, were slated for execution—among them Boudinot's

Stand Watie, along with his brother Elias Boudinot, was a member of the Treaty party and was a Confederate general during the American Civil War.

brother, Stand Watie—but managed to escape.

Watie immediately gathered armed men around him to protect himself and to avenge his kinsmen's deaths. A likely target of Watie's wrath was John Ross, who apparently knew nothing of the plan to execute prominent members of the Treaty party, but whom Watie and others held responsible for the attacks. An armed guard assembled to protect Chief Ross. Then, a council dominated by Ross's supporters quickly voted a pardon for those who had killed the three treaty signers and offered amnesty to members of the Treaty party. Because the amnesty agreement excluded those who accepted it from participation in Cherokee government, Watie and most other Treaty party members declined the offer.

Many Old Settlers realized that civil war threatened, and so they moved to unify the nation. Several of their leaders joined with Ross's followers on September 6, 1839, in drafting a new constitution closely resembling the one written in 1827 in the East. Under this constitution, Ross was elected principal chief and Old Settlers occupied other important offices. Some Old Settlers, however, refused to recognize Ross's leadership and the government established under the Constitution of 1839.

U.S. officials aggravated the situation by continuing to recognize three distinct groups of Cherokees—the Old Settlers, the Treaty party, and the National party—although a majority of Cherokees supported the Constitution of 1839. The Office of Indian Affairs, established in 1824, accepted delegations from various factions and the U.S. agent to the Cherokees gave all of them a hearing. This encouraged the Old Settlers and the Treaty party to oppose a resolution to the discord, particularly one that would confer a minority status on them.

For seven years, intermittent war raged among the Cherokees. Some of those who rebelled against a unified nation, such as Stand Watie and other signers of the New Echota treaty, also sought to avenge the deaths of kinsmen, thereby increasing the bloodshed. Some Cherokees became little more than outlaws. For example, Tom Starr and his brothers claimed to want only to protect the life of their father (who opposed the new national government), but murder and robbery soon became a way of life for them. They terrorized the Cherokee nation until 1848 when the leaders of the gang were killed.

The civil war finally came to an end in 1846 when Ross, Watie, and other Cherokee leaders agreed to a treaty. The treaty pardoned all Cherokees who had committed crimes and created a united Cherokee nation. The treaty did not mean that all past conflicts were forgotten, but the Cherokees in the West were now officially one people.

The Cherokee nation continued to operate under the Constitution of 1839. The constitution provided for three branches of government—executive, legislative, and judicial. It affirmed the Cherokee practice of holding real estate in common while individuals owned improvements. The constitution also specified that improvements could be sold only to other Cherokees and that anyone moving out of the nation forfeited his rights as a Cherokee.

The coming of peace ushered in a period of remarkable achievement for the Cherokees. Many of the missionaries who had served the principal people in the East had gone west, where they helped the Cherokees re-establish churches and mission schools. Samuel A. Worcester, finally released from the Georgia penitentiary, continued to work on the translation of the New Testament, hymnals, and other religious material into Cherokee. He had begun this work in the East in collaboration with Elias Boudinot, and now he carried on alone.

In 1844, even before the signing of the peace treaty, the *Cherokee Advocate* began publication. Like its predecessor, the *Cherokee Phoenix*, the *Advocate* printed the laws of the nation, national and international news, and advertisements in both English and Cherokee. Under the editorship of William P. Ross, nephew of the principal chief and a graduate of Princeton University, the *Advocate* carried a motto that expressed Cherokee nationalism and pride, "Our Rights—Our Country—Our Race."

During the 1840s the Cherokees also established a system of public schools. The crowning achievement in education was the building of two seminaries (high schools), one for men and the other for women, which opened their doors in 1851. The Female Seminary was particularly revolutionary. Most Anglo-Americans at the time believed that women were intellectually inferior to men, and so they had few educational opportunities to acquire beyond basic skills. The Cherokee Female Seminary was modeled after Mount Holyoke Female Seminary in Massachusetts (now Mount Holyoke College), perhaps the most radical educational institution at the time, which had been founded in 1837. The president of Mount Holyoke, Mary Lyon, assisted with the curriculum of the Cherokee Female Seminary, and graduates of the eastern women's college served as teachers at the seminary.

Unfortunately, worthy projects such as the seminaries were stymied by the lack of funds. Although the Constitution of 1839 contained a provision for taxation, the Cherokee government did not levy taxes. Instead, the government invested the money it had received as payment for land cessions, and the interest from this money supported the newspaper, schools, and other governmental operations. The problem was that expenditures, while not extravagant, exceeded income. The Cherokees tried to sell the Neutral Lands, an 800,000 acre tract on which no Cherokees lived, but the U.S. government offered them insultingly unfair terms. As the nation's financial situation grew worse, the Cherokees reluctantly suspended publication of the *Advocate* and closed the seminaries. They would not resume operation until after the Civil War.

The Cherokees built homes and farms in their new territory, and many of them prospered. A total population of 21,000 Cherokees had 102,000 acres under cultivation. They owned 240,000 cattle, 20,000 horses and mules, and

(continued on page 73)

THE ENDURING LEGACY OF CHEROKEE CRAFTS

The Cherokee first developed crafts to make useful objects such as baskets, which held corn. Cherokee basket weavers generally relied on split cane as their primary material, sometimes coloring it with natural dyes extracted from roots and nuts. The expertise of weavers was rivaled by that of potters, who often stamped their clay vessels with decorative geometric designs before holding them indirectly over a flame in order to harden them, a process known as "firing." Potters often stoked these fires with dried corn cobs, which produced a black smoke that left markings on the pots.

The Cherokee also fashioned objects that had a ceremonial rather than a practical purpose. Fine handiwork shows in wooden booger masks, which were worn in a ritual dance that caricatured traditional enemies, including the Europeans who invaded their homeland. At peace councils, the Cherokee smoked ornate pipes, trimmed with shells, cloth, or feathers. Although the Cherokee eventually lost their farming villages, they have preserved much of their culture through the traditional legacy of craftsmanship.

A 19th-century wooden calumet, or peace pipe—attached to a stone bowl—is adorned with feathers, cloth, horsehair, and shells.

A 20th-century Cherokee craftsman carves a booger mask.

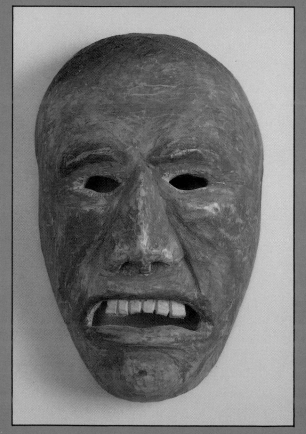

A Cherokee bear's-head mask (above), trimmed with animal fur.

The bared teeth on this wooden booger-mask mock the aggressive grimace of enemy warriors.

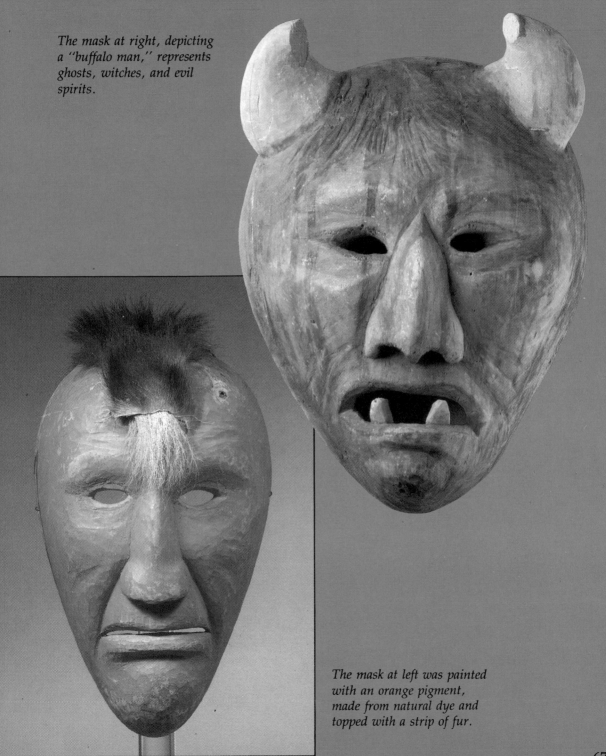

The mask at right, depicting a "buffalo man," represents ghosts, witches, and evil spirits.

The mask at left was painted with an orange pigment, made from natural dye and topped with a strip of fur.

A member of the Eastern Band of Cherokee weaves split cane into a basket.

A 19th-century Cherokee basket (below). The handle is a 20th-century addition.

The 19th-century basket
(above) held dried corn or
beans.

A split-cane jar colored with
dye from bloodroots and
walnuts.

A Cherokee potter readies a clay piece for the kiln, where it will be fired, or baked.

This pot with a "weeping eye" motif (above) dates from the Mississippian period (A.D. 700–1540).

The Mississippian piece (left) bears black markings, created when the pottery was fired over a flame.

A Mississippian pot is decorated with a sculpted frog.

This cooking vessel dates after the Mississippian era. It is stamped with a pattern carved from wood.

These pipes, created for daily rather than ceremonial use, feature human figures carved from soapstone, a soft stone with a gray-green hue.

(continued from page 64)

15,000 hogs. As in the East, the standard of living among the Cherokees varied a great deal. Many of them erected simple one-room cabins and cultivated only a few acres, but others constructed mansions and embarked on lucrative business ventures. Among the most profitable businesses to go into were cattle ranching and salt production. Wealthy Cherokees had clear advantages in settling in Oklahoma: They had capital from the sale of their improvements in the East, and many brought with them their African slaves.

By 1860, Cherokee planters owned 4,000 slaves.

In the period when Cherokees were reestablishing themselves in the West, citizens of the United States were agonizing over the issue of slavery. In November 1860, the conflict over slavery came to a head when a coalition of Southern states, known as the Confederacy, seceded from the Northern states, called the Union, in order to form their own government. This secession led directly to the American Civil War, which erupted in 1861.

The Cherokee Female Seminary opened in 1851. This school was modeled after Mount Holyoke Female Seminary (today Mount Holyoke College), the nation's first school of higher learning for women.

The Civil War placed the Cherokees in an odd position because their laws legitimized the institution of slavery, and their geographical location was in the South. Yet many Cherokees had serious misgivings about slavery, especially the traditionalists, who resented domination by a slaveholding elite. They regarded slavery not necessarily as a moral wrong but as a particularly unsavory feature of the detested Anglo-American culture. In addition, Northern missionaries actively encouraged the abolition of slavery within the United States.

Many slaveholders respected these missionaries and were grateful for the schools and churches they had established, as well as the support they had given the Cherokees during the removal crisis. Furthermore, a number of slaveholders had little desire to ally themselves with the very Southerners who had demanded their removal. In 1861, Chief Ross expressed the Cherokees' dilemma to the council: "Our locality and situation ally us to the South, while to the North we are indebted for a defense of our rights in the past and that enlarged benevolence to which we owe our progress in civilization."

Traditionalists—who favored abolition—and even some slaveholders, such as Ross, preferred neutrality, a position they advocated in order to protect existing treaties between the U.S. government and the Cherokee. In the summer of 1861, Indian nations that neighbored the Cherokee signed treaties with the Confederacy. Because most Cherokee slaveholders favored a Confederate alliance, they encouraged Stand Watie to begin organizing a Cherokee company for the Confederate army. Fearing a division of the nation, John Ross, too, signed a Confederate alliance in August 1861, and Cherokees officially enlisted in the Confederate army.

One of the Cherokee soldiers' initial assignments was to aid in the capture of Opothleyohola, a Creek traditionalist. Opothleyohola opposed the Creeks' Confederate alliance and decided to conduct a group of loyal Creeks, including women and children, to Kansas to take refuge behind Union lines. The Confederacy was determined to stop them. Cherokee traditionalists, in a regiment led by John Drew, refused to fight against fellow Indians whose views on the war they shared. The night before the battle was to take place, they fled their encampment. Some joined Opothleyohola's flight, although others returned to their homes determined to fight for the Confederacy no more.

The Civil War in the United States so divided the Cherokees that they soon became embroiled in a parallel conflict of their own. The Unionist Cherokees, known as "Pins" because their insignia was crossed pins worn under the lapel, attacked Confederate sympathizers and their property. The ardent Confederate Stand Watie and his supporters retaliated. Many Chero-

A dilapidated cabin at Fort Gibson, in Indian Territory, housed slaves owned by a Cherokee.

kees, including Hannah Hicks, the daughter of missionary Samuel A. Worcester, suffered from the repeated assaults of both Confederates and Pins. The Pins killed Hicks's Cherokee husband, a Unionist, by mistake, and Watie's men robbed her house. She wrote in her diary: "Alas, alas, for this miserable people, destroying each other as fast as they can." So many adult Cherokees died in this fighting that the construction of an orphanage became a priority after the war ended.

In the summer of 1862 federal forces invaded the Cherokee nation. They took John Ross captive, but federal authorities soon paroled him, and the principal chief went east to spend the remainder of the war in Washington and Philadelphia. Ross's support of the Confederacy had always been lukewarm at best, and he now became an advocate of Cherokee loyalty to the Union. Although Ross himself was too old to enlist, three of his sons, three grandsons, and three nephews served in the U.S. Army during the Civil War.

When Ross left the nation, Stand Watie saw an opportunity to redress old grievances. He promptly declared the office of principal chief vacant and assumed the position himself. Other

Cherokee officials who had shifted their allegiance to the Union were removed from office and replaced by Watie men. This new government passed a conscription law and began drafting men into Confederate service. This meant that many men who had hoped to remain neutral during the Civil War were forced into hiding in order to avoid fighting for a cause they opposed in their hearts. While the men stayed in hiding, their families keenly felt the loss of their main breadwinner and suffered terrible poverty.

The majority of Cherokees refused to recognize the government headed by Watie and continued to regard Ross as principal chief. These dissenters met in council, revoked the Confederate treaty, and emancipated the slaves. Most slaveholders, however, had already moved their slaves south into the Choctaw nation or northern Texas so this act freed few slaves.

The Civil War ended on April 9, 1865, when Confederate general Robert E. Lee surrendered to Union general Ulysses Grant in Appomattox, Virginia.

The flag of the Keetowah Society, whose members were Union sympathizers.

But conflict continued within the Cherokee nation until June 1865, when Brigadier General Stand Watie became the last Confederate general to surrender. This surrender did not, however, insure a united Cherokee nation.

When the Cherokee Union and Confederate representatives met with United States peace commissioners, the commissioners insisted that *all* Cherokees had been supporters of the Confederacy. Furthermore, they refused to recognize Ross as principal chief. In fact, Watie and the Confederate Cherokees received a far more cordial reception than Ross and the loyal Cherokees.

One reason for this new friendship was the willingness of the Confederate Cherokees to grant American railroad companies rights of way across the Cherokee nation. In order to secure those rights of way, the United States seemed agreeable to a proposed division of the Cherokee nation in which the railroads could lay tracks in the land "controlled" by Watie. How ironic it seemed to Ross that the United States had fought a war to preserve the Union only to permit a secession by southern Cherokees.

In the end, the Cherokees preserved their nation and signed a treaty on August 11, 1865. The agreement extended citizenship rights to the freed slaves, permitted Delawares and Shawnees—Native American peoples—to settle on Cherokee land, ceded the Neutral Lands to the United States, and granted rights-of-way to railroads.

The railroad rights-of-way spelled doom for the Cherokee nation. Railroads competed to complete their lines through the Cherokee nation both to gain access to the cattle markets in Texas and to obtain sections of land along the construction routes. In the late 19th century, the U.S. government helped fund railroad construction by granting sections of public land to the railroads. Once the tracks had been laid, the line established, and the towns built along the route, land values along the railroad skyrocketed. The railroads could then sell the land to help defray construction costs.

In the Cherokee nation, however, public land did not belong to the United States but was held in common by the Cherokees. By promising the railroads free tracts of land, the U.S. government was giving away property that it did not own. The railroads could take possession of this territory only when the Indian title was extinguished, and the land reverted to the United States. Thus the railroad owners, some of the wealthiest and most powerful men in America, came to view the Cherokee nation as an obstacle to the reaping of additional profits and as an impediment to progress.

These wealthy industrialists were not alone in coveting Cherokee territory. The passage of the Homestead Act in 1862 gave many landless people in the United States hope of acquiring western property. This law awarded 160 acres for a nominal fee to anyone who settled and cultivated unoccupied lots for at least 5 years. Rapid population growth in the United States after the Civil War made whites eager to take advantage of the Homestead Act. They saw in Indian real estate, particularly in what is today Oklahoma, an opportunity for expansion and flooded into the Oklahoma territory, homesteading on ceded Indian tracts, such as the Cherokee Strip. These whites felt that they were justified in taking over Indian land because the Cherokees and other native peoples had far more acreage than they seemed to need or deserve.

Whites poured into the Cherokee nation as laborers on railroads and as workers in other enterprises, such as mining and logging. This created a chaotic situation because white people were not subject to the laws of the Cherokee nation. Federal marshals tried to

These Confederate Cherokee delegates journeyed to Washington in 1866 to negotiate a treaty that would divide the Cherokee nation into two factions. The tribe ultimately remained unified. The delegation included (left to right) John Rollin Ridge, grandson of Major Ridge; Saladin Watie, son of Stand Watie; Judge Richard Fields; Elias Cornelius Boudinot; and William Penn Adair.

The first train arrives in Tahlequah, Oklahoma. When the Cherokee granted rights-of-way to the railroads, companies immediately began competing to lay tracks through Indian land.

keep the peace, but they were over-worked and resented. The turmoil made the Cherokee nation a haven for outlaws and led many people to support the extension of United States law over Indian territory, thus bringing Indian governments to an end.

A new generation of philanthropists, influenced by those who had once prescribed the civilization program as the antidote to Indian troubles, expressed their distress that native peoples seemed to be as attached to their own nations and ways of life as ever. In the name of "saving the Cherokee" they began to advocate assimilation once again. The best method to accomplish this goal seemed to be the termination of tribal ownership of land and the allotment of 160-acre tracts to individuals. "Surplus" land would be opened to white settlement. These "friends of the Indian" believed that if each person had a privately owned farm, he would soon abandon his Indian ways and become culturally indistinguishable from white Americans. Because most native peoples held their land in common and their governments rested on that principle, a division of Indian land would bring about an end to Indian nations. Railroad companies, of course, supported the dissolution of Indian governments, including the Cherokee nation, knowing that they stood to gain valuable title to the Cherokee land grants. White homesteaders anticipated carving farms out of the remaining territory the railroads did not want.

Unable to resist economic and "philanthropic" pressure, the U.S. Congress passed the General Allotment Act in 1887, often called the Dawes Act after its sponsor, Henry L. Dawes. This legislation divided up Indian land once

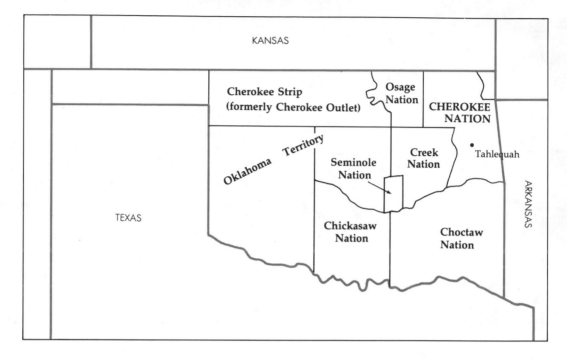

held in common by native peoples, allotted it to them as individuals, opened surplus land to white settlement, and brought Indian peoples under federal jurisdiction. In order to offer some protection to traditionalists, who were unaccustomed to private land ownership, the act restricted sale of individual allotments for 25 years.

The Dawes Act exempted the Cherokees and a few other groups from allotment, but in 1893 Congress directed President Grover Cleveland to appoint commissioners to negotiate allotment agreements with those peoples. During the next three years, Congress authorized the survey of Indian land and the compilation of "official rolls," lists of those Indians entitled to receive allotments. The Cherokees steadfastly re-

fused to negotiate, but they could do little else to resist allotment.

The Cherokees were handicapped in their resistance because their national treasury was empty. After the Civil War, the Cherokees had supported their nation by leasing the Cherokee Strip (or Outlet) to white ranchers. In 1890 the U.S. government closed the Strip to cattlemen, and the Cherokee government lost its major source of income. In 1893 the Cherokees were compelled to sell the land to the United States for $1.40 per acre, and the Strip was opened to white settlement under the provisions of the Homestead Act.

The Cherokees continued to oppose allotment and refused to cooperate with the Dawes Commission when it arrived to prepare the official Cherokee roll.

Congress authorized the commission to continue without tribal cooperation. When Cherokees refused to appear before the commission to select their allotments, the commission assigned plots of land to them. Finally, in the Curtis Act of 1898, Congress ended Indian land tenure without the Indians' consent in preparation for the admission of the state of Oklahoma to the Union in 1907. Having no real alternative, the practically defunct Cherokee nation agreed to allotment in 1902, virtually after the fact. Although the Cherokee nation in the West continued with a chief appointed by the president of the United States, all remnants of sovereignty were gone.

The Cherokees and other native peoples who originally lived in the South (often called "the five civilized tribes") opposed the creation of the state of Oklahoma. In 1905 representatives of these Indian nations drafted a constitution for a proposed Indian state to be called Sequoyah. The state included the land of these Indian nations in the eastern half of what was to become Oklahoma. Congress tabled the constitution, thereby rejecting the admission of Sequoyah to the Union.

In 1907, the state of Oklahoma was admitted to the Union. As part of the celebration a mock wedding took place between an Indian woman and a cowboy, symbolizing the marriage of two cultures. This ceremony was not an accurate representation of Oklahoma statehood. Indians, who had once held title to the entire state, were now a minority. Their own nations, laws, and customs abolished, Indians found themselves dominated and exploited. Contrary to the hopes of capitalists and philanthropists, however, the Cherokees and other native peoples in Oklahoma did not disappear nor, in fact, did their traditions and values. ▲

Climbing Bear of the Eastern Band of Cherokee was photographed by anthropologist James Mooney in 1888.

THE
EASTERN BAND
OF
CHEROKEES

Not all Cherokees living in the East traveled the Trail of Tears west of the Mississippi in the early 19th century. After removal, a community of Cherokees numbering approximately 1,000 remained behind in the remote mountains of western North Carolina. These people came to be known as the Eastern Band of Cherokee Indians. They traced their origins to the Treaty of 1819, which permitted Cherokees living within ceded territory to register for individual reservations of 640 acres and become American citizens.

Forty-nine families in North Carolina chose to remain on their land rather than move across the Little Tennessee River, which had become the boundary of the Cherokee nation. These Cherokees felt little regret over severing their formal ties to the Cherokee nation and becoming citizens of the state of North Carolina. In many ways, they had resisted changes in their traditional way of life. The "civilization" program of the U.S. government and the Christianization efforts of missionaries had had relatively little impact on them. They preferred traditional government, education, and religion and reviled a republican government, Christianity, and mission schools—all advocated by the leaders of the Cherokee nation. Most of all, they wanted to continue to hunt in the forests where Kana'ti had found game, to farm the fields darkened by Selu's blood, and to fish in the rivers that had given birth to Wild Boy.

Unfortunately, these Cherokees experienced the same difficulties as others who received reservations under the terms of the Treaty of 1819. North Carolina had already sold the reservations granted to the eastern Cherokees by the federal government. North Carolina, however, admitted the error and paid the Cherokees for their land. A few Cherokees, including Euchella, a prominent local leader, took the money and moved their families across the Little

Tennessee into the Cherokee nation. Others, however, chose to stay in North Carolina. Under the leadership of Yonaguska, they settled along the Oconaluftee River and supported themselves by selling livestock and ginseng, a medicinal herb, to white traders.

The Oconaluftee Cherokees, as they were known in the early 19th century, had little experience dealing with the non-Cherokee world. Few spoke English or had other skills necessary for protecting their land and themselves from whites who hungrily eyed their territory. Fortunately, they found a spokesman in William Holland Thomas, a fatherless white boy whom Yonaguska had adopted. When he grew up, Thomas became a trader, and he helped the Cherokees consolidate their landholdings by purchasing tracts for them as the land became available. When the removal treaty was signed in 1835, the Oconaluftee Cherokees insisted that it did not apply to them because they were no longer part of the Cherokee nation. Instead they were citizens of North Carolina. Thomas went to Washington, D.C., to lobby on their behalf and pleaded their case before the North Carolina legislature.

In the end, his efforts helped save the Oconaluftee Cherokees from removal. North Carolina tacitly assented to their remaining in the state, and the United States also informally recognized their rights under earlier treaties. Nevertheless, the position of the Oconaluftee Cherokees was precarious. Although they had considerable sympathy for those Cherokees who were being hunted by soldiers, imprisoned in stockades, and marched off to the West, any aid to the victims jeopardized their own status.

Tension increased when citizens of the Cherokee nation, a man named Tsali and his sons, killed two soldiers involved in the Cherokee roundup and wounded another. They then fled with their wives and children into the mountains. General Winfield Scott insisted that these Cherokees must be punished. In order to secure their own position, the Oconaluftee Cherokees agreed to assist in the capture of Tsali's band.

Thomas and the Oconaluftees enlisted the aid of Euchella, Yonaguska's son-in-law, who was subject to removal because he had moved back into the Cherokee nation. These Cherokees captured Tsali's band and executed the murderers. Oral tradition suggests that they did this reluctantly and that Tsali recognized the necessity of their actions and faced his executioners courageously. Because of his assistance in capturing Tsali's band, Euchella received permission to remain with the Oconaluftee Cherokees. General Scott also withdrew the soldiers and, thus, other fugitives were able to come out of hiding. More than 1,000 Cherokees managed to remain in North Carolina.

The descendants of fugitives, Euchella, and the Oconaluftees became the Eastern Band of Cherokees. They forged a common identity, in part by retelling the story of Tsali, a Cherokee who loved his country so much that he was willing to kill rather than leave and who willingly died so that other Cherokees could remain in their homeland. Although many versions of the account do not bear up under close historical scrutiny, Tsali has become a folk hero who embodies the deep attachment eastern Cherokees feel for their land.

The desire to remain in the East recurs as a theme throughout the history of the Eastern Band. Nevertheless, the federal government made periodic attempts to convince them to join their relatives in the West. These attempts usually stemmed from the government's desire to clarify the status of the Cherokees or to simplify the administration of Indian policy. Occasionally, groups of Cherokees went west looking for better opportunities or escaping political factionalism at home. Most eastern Cherokees, however, were determined to stay exactly where they were.

After removal, the lives of eastern Cherokees changed little until the Civil War. William H. Thomas was an enthusiastic supporter of the Confederacy, and he convinced more than 200 Cherokees to enlist in a legion he was organizing for the Confederate army.

A typical house of the eastern Cherokees in North Carolina in 1908.

William Holland Thomas was an orphan when he was adopted by Yonaguska, a Cherokee leader. Thomas became an interpreter and trader and remained a loyal friend to the Cherokees.

Joining Thomas out of personal commitment rather than political sentiments, the Cherokees primarily did defensive duty in eastern Tennessee and western North Carolina. In 1864 a Union force captured between 20 and 30 members of Thomas's legion.

In a prison camp in Knoxville, Tennessee, many of these Cherokees learned for the first time that they had been defending the right of the South to uphold slavery. Some prisoners, owning no slaves and having little sympathy for wealthy planters, renounced their allegiance to the Confederacy. When they received federal pardons, they joined the Union army. A few Cherokees, therefore, were veterans of both the Confederate and Union armies. When they returned home after the war, they encountered considerable hostility from those who remained loyal to Thomas and his legion.

The period of Reconstruction immediately following the Civil War brought major changes to the Cherokee people. Under the newly devised Reconstruction constitution of North Carolina, they acquired the right to vote, and some began to exercise that right in the counties where they lived. In 1868 the Cherokees also wrote their own constitution and, despite considerable factionalism, elected a chief and council. In the same year, the federal government recognized the eastern Cherokees as an Indian tribe distinct from the western Cherokees.

At this point, the Cherokees certainly needed the protection that a formal political system and federal recognition would help ensure. William Holland Thomas had suffered severe business reverses as a result of the war, and his health failed. Thomas's creditors began to seize his property. Unfortunately, Thomas held title to land he had bought for the Cherokees, but his illness prevented him from sorting out who actually owned what. His creditors, of course, assumed that property in Thomas' name belonged to him and seized it in payment of his debts. Some of the land, however, had already been paid for by the Cherokees, although the deed had not yet been assigned to them.

The United States instituted a lawsuit on behalf of the Cherokees. The court awarded much of the land in question to the Cherokees, and the federal government accepted the title in trust. This meant that the Cherokees owned the land but could not sell it without federal approval. Although more acculturated Cherokees sometimes resented federal control of their land, the trusteeship offered the eastern Cherokees some protection from land-hungry whites who were beginning to show interest in the Indians' rugged mountain homeland.

The Cherokees' new relationship with the federal government brought a number of social changes, particularly in education. Before the Civil War parents taught their children the Sequoyah syllabary at home, but few children received a formal English-language education. After the war, the United States arranged for a few students to attend boarding school, but many became homesick, particularly when racial prejudice led whites in the schools to treat them as inferiors.

In 1881, Quakers from Indiana contracted with the Eastern Band to provide a school system. They established day schools in several communities and a boarding school in what is today the town of Cherokee, North Carolina. This arrangement sparked a controversy that centered around the Quakers' political leanings. In 1892, the federal government took over the educational system.

Both Quakers and federal teachers attempted to eradicate traditional Cherokee practices and beliefs among their students. They forced Cherokees to speak English and washed children's mouths out with soap if they used their native language. Only decades later did the education system come to value the Cherokees' own heritage.

The attempt to destroy Cherokee culture and assimilate native people was no more successful in North Carolina than it was in Oklahoma. Many Cherokees found their way of life preferable to that of white Americans and sought to preserve it, accepting change when they could carefully direct it. For example, the Cherokees no longer had independent villages with councils. Instead they established the *gadugi*, or work company, defined by anthropologist John Witthoft as "the social survival of the Cherokee town, carrying on the economic functions of the town long after its political functions were lost."

Members of the gadugi worked together on each person's land, and if someone was sick, the gadugi did his work for him. The gadugi also worked for nonmembers and used the proceeds from their labors to fund various projects or to pay for members' funerals. The gadugi embodied the communal values of traditional Cherokee culture and applied them to the modern world.

Swimmer, a Cherokee medicine man of considerable ability, also represented continuity between the past and the future. For more than a decade before his death in 1899, Swimmer shared his knowledge with anthropologist James Mooney. Mooney recorded Swimmer's stories about how the earth was made and about Kana'ti and Selu. Swimmer also revealed to Mooney his sacred formulas. These were prescriptions for illness, charms for hunting, and love potions that he carefully had

The Cherokee medicine man Swimmer played a crucial role in the preservation of his native culture by relating Cherokee myths and sacred formulas to anthropologist James Mooney.

recorded in the Sequoyah syllabary. Swimmer permitted Mooney to present them to the Smithsonian Institution in Washington, D.C., because he feared that they otherwise might be lost to a younger generation who no longer valued traditional ways.

Although traditional culture remained strong, Cherokee leaders in the post–Civil War period were more adept at dealing with the non-Cherokee world than their predecessors had been. They began to look for ways to expand the tribal domain and services. One possible source of funds was money derived from the sale of the Neutral Lands in the West. The eastern Cherokees sued their western brothers for a share in the proceeds of the sale. In 1886 the U.S. Supreme Court ruled that the Cherokees had severed their formal ties to the Cherokee nation in their refusal to emigrate west and had no right to share in the nation's income. The Court went on to state that the eastern Cherokees did not, in fact, compose a tribe but were instead merely citizens of the state of North Carolina. This ruling caused the Cherokees considerable consternation. They were disappointed that no moneys would be forthcoming, but more alarming was the Court's ruling that they were not a tribe.

Confusion stemming from the Court ruling engulfed the eastern Cherokees just as politically powerful whites in North Carolina began raising objections to the Indians' maintaining rights of citizenship. The state's dominant party, the Democrats, had always counted on the Cherokees' allegiance at election time. Their loyalty went unquestioned until 1884, when the Eastern Band unexpectedly shifted to the Republican side and cast their votes for James G. Blaine, the Republican nominee in the presidential election of that year.

North Carolina Democrats saw the Cherokees' support of a Republican candidate as a slap in the face. The Cherokees' hold on the balance of power between the two parties in local counties exacerbated the situation. North Carolina Democrats looked for ways to disfranchise the Cherokees, thus jeopardizing their legal status. Were they really citizens of the state? Were they entitled to enjoy the privileges of citizenship, such as voting? Or were they merely wards of the federal government, which held their lands in trust and administered their affairs? The Supreme Court had suggested that the Cherokees in the East did not constitute a tribe, yet the federal government treated the Eastern Band as though it were a tribe.

The eastern Cherokee chief in the 1880s, Nimrod Jarrett Smith, countered these threats with an ingenious move that gave the Cherokees a definite legal status and some protection under state law. He applied to the North Carolina legislature for a corporate charter, which was awarded in 1889. This charter made the Eastern Band of Cherokee Indians a corporation. As such, they could enter into contracts, own prop-

James Mooney studied and recorded the culture and history of the Cherokees. He described their 1838 removal in Myths of the Cherokee, *published in 1900.*

erty, manage their assets, and bring suit in court. The corporate charter gave the Cherokees considerable protection in an age when the rights of corporations were regarded as almost inviolable. The charter provided for the administration of the corporation, and it is under this charter (with a few revisions and modifications) that the eastern Cherokees have governed themselves ever since.

The corporate charter did not, however, end the Cherokees' problems. The tribal council faced serious difficulties with property taxes owed to the coun-

North Carolina Cherokee women in traditional dress. In the early 20th century, the Eastern Band struggled to preserve its heritage and homeland in the face of opposition from federal and state governments.

ties in which it held land. One way of paying outstanding taxes and redeeming land already seized for nonpayment was selling timber on tribal land. The council, acting as a corporation, entered into a contract for sale of the timber. The federal government, treating Cherokees as wards, made other arrangements for the sale of the timber. Ultimately the case ended up in court. In 1895, a federal court ruled that the Indians were indeed wards, not citizens, and that they could not sell their timber independently.

Although the timber transaction ultimately was resolved satisfactorily, the case had far-reaching effects for the Cherokees. Democrats, who were a majority in North Carolina, remembered the Republican votes cast by the Cherokees. Democratic politicians decided that if the Cherokees were wards and not citizens, then they could no longer vote. In 1900 the state refused to permit

Cherokees to vote; they did not regain that right until 1930.

The timber sale took place at the very same time that the U.S. Congress provided for the allotment of Indian land to individuals, in effect ending Indian governments. The federal government was in the process of forcing allotment on the western Cherokees. Many people in North Carolina expected the same policy to be applied to the Eastern Band with tracts of land *and* proceeds from the timber sale going to individuals. In anticipation of the division of Cherokee funds among members of the band, many whites deceitfully managed to get their names on the official roll. They were disappointed: Allotment did not come to the Eastern Band. Nevertheless, these "white Cherokees" benefited from their enrollment, frequently at the expense of true Cherokees. Federal trusteeship prevented non-Cherokees from buying Cherokee land, but this provision did not apply to "white Cherokees," who soon came to dominate the economic life of the Eastern Band, becoming prominent figures in Cherokee politics as well.

The Eastern Band entered the 20th century as a far more diverse group than they had been when they escaped removal to the West. No longer isolated from the dominant American culture, they struggled to protect their land and their society from the world at large, and from the internal disharmony that plagued them. As the Eastern Band moved into the 20th century, they asked themselves if they could survive in the modern world. ▲

Wilma Mankiller became the Cherokees' principal chief in 1985.

CHEROKEES
IN THE
20TH CENTURY

By the early 20th century, the Cherokees had become extremely diverse. They lived in Oklahoma and North Carolina, separated by half a continent. Some Cherokees had embraced the message of missionaries and philanthropists, and they had assimilated into the dominant American culture. They called themselves "Cherokee," but they meant only that their ancestry, and not their culture, was Cherokee. Other people, including black freedmen and "white Cherokees," had dubious claims to Cherokee ancestry, yet the appearance of their names on official rolls made them legally Cherokees.

Still other Cherokees based their ethnic identity on both ancestry and culture. Although some aspects of their lives had changed, these Cherokees preferred their own language, values, and religion to those of the dominant culture. Sometimes these traditionalists were derided and even exploited by assimilated Cherokees. In recent decades, however, a respect and appreciation for

traditionalists has been rekindled, and the survival of Cherokee culture has become a source of strength and pride for all of the principal people.

In the West, the United States forced allotment on the Cherokees at the turn of the 20th century. Although the Cherokee nation opposed allotment, many individuals with Cherokee ancestry of questionable authenticity got their names on the official roll, advocated the policy, and received allotments. In the end, most assimilated Cherokees came to accept the policy, settle on their allotments, and participate in the new state of Oklahoma.

The Cherokee Robert Latham Owen was one of the first two Oklahomans elected to the U.S. Senate in 1907. Such individuals identified with the principal people only because their ancestors were Cherokees and their names were on the official roll. Nothing else in their way of life distinguished them from white Oklahomans. Despite their apathy toward their own ancestry, these

Cherokees came to represent the remnants of the Cherokee nation.

After the virtual suspension of the Cherokee government by the Curtis Act in 1898, the president of the United States began appointing the Cherokee chief, and the chief chose all other Cherokee officials. Presidents selected assimilated Cherokees such as W. W. Keeler, who was appointed chief by Harry Truman. Keeler, the president of Phillips Petroleum, was a man more comfortable at the White House than at the stomp ground (a ceremonial site still used for traditional rituals such as the Green Corn Ceremony).

Many western Cherokees, however, preferred the stomp ground. They felt estranged from the new state and from the Cherokees who had accepted a role in it. Under the leadership of Red Bird Smith these people turned to an ancient religious society, the Keetoowah, for guidance and organized their own council. Red Bird Smith's son later recalled the reaction of these Cherokees: "At that time the Cherokees were being oppressed from all sides, their confidence betrayed by the people in which they had placed their greatest trust. My father and other old members of the council were seriously depressed. Their only hope to survive was through the power that lives behind the sun."

Retreating into the hills of eastern Oklahoma, members of the Keetoowah took spiritual refuge in traditional beliefs. They refused to accept allotments, live on tracts assigned to them, or have anything to do with the new political and economic order.

Other Oklahoman residents generally showed interest in these people only when an opportunity to exploit them surfaced. For example, many traditionalists became the victims of unscrupulous individuals who had themselves appointed "guardians" for the estates of Indians who could not or would not manage their allotments. The discovery of oil on allotments previously thought to be of little value (and consequently assigned to traditionalists) led to gross abuses of the office of guardian. Many Indians were defrauded of their estates by people who were supposed to be their protectors. Kate Barnard, commissioner of Oklahoma's Office of Charities and Corrections, was one of the few public officials to recognize and speak out against the abuses of guardians:

> I have been compelled to see orphans robbed, starved, and buried for money. I have named the men and accused them and furnished the records and affadavits to convict them, but with no result. I decided long ago that Oklahoma had no citizen who cared whether or not an orphan is robbed or starved or killed—because his dead claim is easier to handle than if he were alive.

The swindles of guardians contributed dramatically to the loss of Indian land. In 1891 western Cherokees had owned 19,500,000 acres; by 1971 Cher-

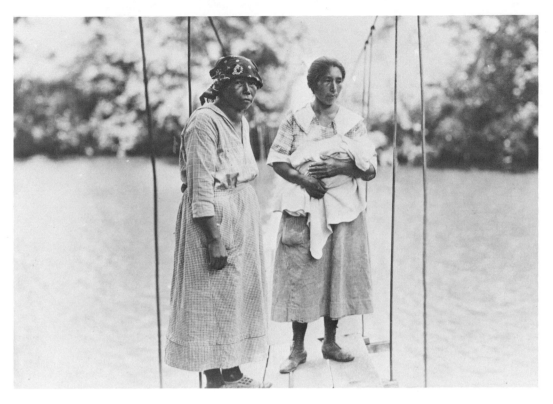

Two female members of the Eastern Band pose for a photographer in about 1930.

okees held only 146,598 acres in Oklahoma.

The much smaller Eastern Band of Cherokees managed to keep a land base of more than 56,000 acres in western North Carolina. Most Cherokees lived in Qualla Boundary, a 44,000-acre tract in Jackson and Swain counties, but others lived nearby on scattered parcels in Swain, Cherokee, and Graham counties. Despite their extensive holdings, the political and economic position of the Eastern Band remained precarious. Disfranchised by the state in 1900, the eastern Cherokees hoped that their right to vote would be automatically restored when in 1924 the federal government extended citizenship rights to all Native Americans who had not previously enjoyed them. But North Carolina officials insisted that members of the Eastern Band could not be made citizens until their land had been allotted. Finally, in 1930, Congress passed "an Act to confer full rights of citizenship upon the Cherokee Indians resident in the State of North Carolina." Yet even this precise language did not

THE QUALLA BOUNDARY AND SURROUNDING AREA

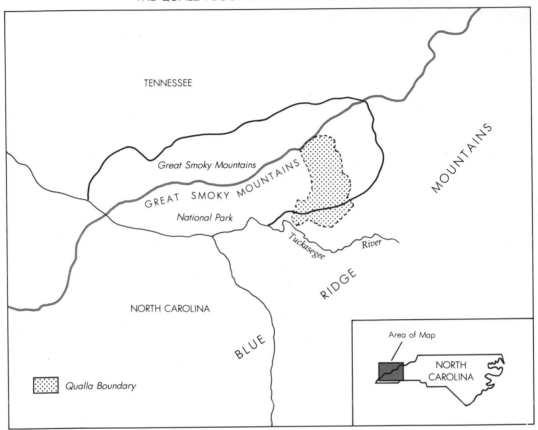

TENNESSEE

Great Smoky Mountains

GREAT SMOKY MOUNTAINS

National Park

MOUNTAINS

Tuckasegee River

RIDGE

NORTH CAROLINA

BLUE

Qualla Boundary

Area of Map

NORTH CAROLINA

convince local county election boards that the Cherokees enjoyed the right of suffrage, and few Cherokees were allowed to register to vote before World War II.

In the early 20th century, the timber industry and related enterprises dominated the economy of western North Carolina. The Cherokees had sold their best timber at the end of the 19th century, but the sale of pulp wood and tanbark continued into the 1920s and provided employment for some Cherokees. Although they benefited from

steady employment, the Cherokees suffered prejudice and discrimination. According to anthropologist John Witthoft, Cherokee workers received only 35 cents a day while whites were paid $1 a day.

When the timber boom ended in the mid-1920s, the Cherokees found themselves without any prospect of future employment. Furthermore, the dramatic increase in the Cherokee population at the turn of the 20th century—produced by the enrollment of avaricious whites onto official rolls—

strained resources. "White Cherokees" had come to control the Eastern Band's most fertile land, pushing traditionalists into remote coves or onto treeless, eroded hillsides. Reduced to subsistence farming, many barely survived. Their living conditions deteriorated throughout the decade. In 1932 during the Great Depression, a census taker visited Qualla Boundary and reported on the condition of a family there:

> [The house] was worse than filthy; no furnishings, and not fit for a hog pen—garbage knee deep about the house; offensive odor; human waste all about . . . flies in droves; sanitation uncared for. . . . I don't see how they live and they are not living, but just existing.

By the mid-1930s the New Deal, an economic reform program introduced by President Franklin D. Roosevelt, had brought some relief to the Eastern Band. Cherokees participated in various work-relief programs, including the Works Progress Administration and the National Youth Administration. In addition, approximately 100 Cherokee men received 2 weeks of work per month from the Indian Emergency Conservation Work Program. This program focused on conserving natural resources, and projects in western North Carolina included the improvement of roads and the construction of horse and truck trails.

The opening of the Great Smoky Mountains National Park in 1934 was a

The booming timber industry provided employment for many Cherokees in North Carolina until the mid-1920s.

momentous event for the Eastern Band. The federal government believed that the Indians of Qualla Boundary, which adjoined the park, could serve as a tourist attraction and originally intended to integrate them into the park. When the Cherokees successfully resisted this plan, the government helped native artisans organize a cooperative to market their baskets, pottery, woodcarvings, and other crafts.

The park brought thousands of tourists to the region and gave the Eastern Band a new source of income through

President Franklin Roosevelt opens the Great Smoky Mountains National Park in 1934. Cherokees relied on the tourism generated by the park to provide them with a steady source of income.

the sale of souvenirs. The influx of whites also permanently changed the lives of the eastern Cherokees by thrusting them into daily contact with Americans from across the country. By the late 1980s, more people visited the Great Smoky Mountains than any other national park, entering the park through Qualla Boundary.

The Roosevelt administration's impact on the Cherokees was not limited to New Deal programs and the opening of the park. In 1933 the president appointed John Collier, a sociologist with a long history of defending Indian rights, to the post of Commissioner of Indian Affairs. Collier secured passage of the Indian Reorganization Act (IRA), also known as the Wheeler-Howard Act, which officially recognized that the allotment program had been a disaster for native peoples. This legislation ended the process of allotment, banned the unregulated sale of Indian lands, and authorized the appropriation of $2 million a year to purchase land for Indians. The act also permitted the organization of Indian governments and sanctioned the incorporation of native peoples. These provisions made it possible for Indians to direct their own economic development and to appear as a body in court. Collier viewed the bill as "the beginning in the process of liberating and rejuvenating a subjugated and exploited race in the midst of an aggressive civilization."

Although the Indian Reorganization Act set a beneficial new tone for Indian relations with the federal government, the legislation had little actual effect on the principal people in the East or in the West. In the East, the act's condemnation of allotment angered many "white Cherokees" who had hoped to profit from the dissolution of the Eastern Band's land base. They continued to promote individual ownership of land. This produced deep factionalism among the eastern Cherokees because traditionalists tended to favor their communal land system, which Collier sought to protect.

Because of political pressure from whites and assimilated Indians in Oklahoma, the Indian Reorganization Act overlooked the western Cherokees and other native peoples in that state. In 1936, however, Congress passed the Oklahoma Indian Welfare Act, which gave Indians the right to adopt constitutions and secure corporate charters. This legislation provided for the federal purchase of land to be held in trust for incorporated Oklahoma Indians. The government also made loans to various Indian economic development projects, including one promising scheme to grow and market strawberries. Yet by 1936, the Cherokee population of eastern Oklahoma had scattered, making impossible the dream of an Indian nation with a communally owned land base.

New Deal programs brought less prosperity to western Cherokee traditionalists than to their relatives in the East. No equivalent of the Great Smoky Mountains National Park promised a long-term solution to their economic problems. Nevertheless, agricultural agents—funded by the federal government—introduced scientific farming techniques, and home-demonstration agents, their female counterparts, instructed women in food preparation, hygiene, and child care. New school programs provided educational opportunities for Indian children. Poverty in many Cherokee communities, how-

ever, was so profound that these measures had limited impact.

World War II did bring significant changes to the Cherokees. As in World War I, many Cherokees enlisted in the armed forces. Historian John R. Finger has demonstrated how the experience of the Great War took a generation of young Cherokees beyond the circumscribed world of their Indian communities and introduced them not only to a broader American society but also to that of Europe. Similarly, in World War II, well more than a thousand Cherokees fought alongside fellow Americans of all races and ethnicities. Some had been drafted by the armed forces, but the majority had volunteered. After the war, the G.I. Bill helped many Cherokee veterans to attend college free of charge. Furthermore, in 1946 Cherokee veterans in North Carolina finally forced county registrars to permit them to vote.

By the 1950s, many Cherokees had broadened their horizons and left reservations in order to move into urban centers throughout the United States. This shift from the country to the city resulted from a federal relocation program instituted by the Bureau of Indian Affairs. The bureau instituted job training programs in industrial cities, sometimes offering to teach Indians directly, sometimes paying their tuition at a vocational school. The "new" policy of drawing Indians from reservations in fact reflected a philosophy—operative since the 19th century—that Native

Americans would fare best by moving into mainstream society.

As in the past, the federal program of the 1950s met with both praise and criticism. Advocates of relocation argued that by leaving their enclaves Indians would gain the same economic opportunities that other Americans enjoyed. The policy's detractors accused the government of acting out of self-interest. They asserted that the United States cared little about Indian welfare and wanted to move Native Americans into cities in order to reduce the cost of administering federally sponsored programs on the reservations. Indeed, many tribes suffered terribly upon entering cities because they lost many of the benefits, such as free health care and education, that the government had once provided. The Oklahoma Cherokees, in particular, fell on hard times. Many moved off reservations and into urban slums where they worked at menial jobs and suffered racial discrimination from whites.

The overall economic conditions for the Cherokees living in North Carolina and Oklahoma slowly began to improve in the 1950s and 1960s, largely through the aid of community action programs. The Eastern Band established the Cherokee Tribal Community Services program in 1952 and imposed a sales tax to finance fire and police protection, garbage collection, and sewer and water lines. The western Cherokees found funds to finance their own development in 1961 when the Indians

Claims Commission, which had been established in 1946 to settle claims against the U.S. government, awarded them $15 million for the forced sale of the Cherokee Strip in 1893 to the federal government. Although the money was paid on a per capita basis to descendants of Cherokees on the official roll, the payments of those who had no heirs or could not be located went to the Cherokee nation and helped finance the construction of a cultural center and land purchases.

Self-help projects found additional stimulus in the Great Society programs devised by the Johnson administration in the 1960s to end poverty in America. The Eastern Band, for example, obtained funding to build and refurbish housing. According to John Witthoft, in 1946, 90 percent of the houses on Qualla Boundary were hardly fit for people to live in. By the 1970s, substandard housing had been reduced to 50 percent—not an enviable percentage but certainly an improvement. Among the western Cherokees also, federal funds provided better housing and sanitation.

These programs, however, did not entirely solve the problems facing the Cherokees. During the 1960s, deep cultural divisions remained, especially between traditional Oklahoma Cherokees and the assimilated western Cherokees, who held the greatest sway over tribal affairs. Traditional Cherokees, who numbered approximately 11,000 during this period, organized to assert their rights, creating an informal organiza-

At the Cherokee Gardens in Tahlequah, workers inspect plants to ensure their high quality. During the 1970s and 1980s Cherokees founded many independent businesses.

tion, the Five County Northeastern Oklahoma Cherokee Organization, to voice their concerns about economic and cultural exploitation. The movement lasted only from 1965 to 1973, but it succeeded in calling attention to the plight of traditional Cherokees and demanding that Cherokee leaders include them in their development schemes.

Other political changes have occurred among the western Cherokees. In 1970, they voted for principal chief for the first time since Oklahoma statehood, and in 1975 they enacted a new constitution that provided for the election of tribal officials, permanently ending the practice of presidential appointment. The democratization of the western Cherokees gave traditionalists the voice in government that they had been denied since statehood. Although elected officials had relatively little territory over which to preside, the revitalized Cherokee nation was a complex of businesses, programs, and services. By 1987, the Cherokee nation in Oklahoma had 72,000 members and tribal assets of more than $40 million.

New opportunities and a renewed commitment to traditional communities drew many Cherokees back to Oklahoma. One of these was Wilma Mankiller, whose father had relocated to San Francisco when she was a child. In 1975 she came home to Oklahoma. Mankiller became active in development projects, particularly one that brought water to remote traditional Cherokee communities. The Cherokees elected her vice chief and then principal chief of the Cherokee nation. Chief Mankiller, who grew up far away from her Cherokee homeland, embodies a new concern for Cherokee culture and for those people actively preserving it.

Unlike their western brethren, the 8,000 members of the Eastern Band encountered obstacles in their attempts to improve life on their reservation. Because the eastern Cherokees did not have clear title to their land (the federal government held it in trust), businesses were reluctant to invest money within

In the town of Cherokee, North Carolina, high school boys enjoy football practice. Young Cherokees have adapted features of American culture while still embracing their own heritage as the principal people.

Qualla Boundary. This situation retarded economic development and forced many Cherokees to depend on the seasonal tourist industry for their income.

In order to be successful, these Cherokees had to provide tourists with a stereotypical view of Indians, featuring a life-style including tipis and warbonnets—two items Cherokees never traditionally used. In recent years, however, a museum and several other attractions have presented a more authentic account of Cherokee history and culture. Unfortunately, tourism did not solve all the economic problems of the eastern Cherokees. Unemployment continued to soar each winter, and Cherokee incomes in the 1970s were only 60 percent of the national average.

In the 1980s the eastern Cherokees explored innovative and controversial solutions to their economic problems. Qualla Boundary is not subject to state laws prohibiting gambling, and so a group of Cherokee businessmen opened a high-stakes bingo parlor to attract players from throughout the nation. Bingo provided employment for many Cherokees, who could operate the game or work in restaurants and motels providing accommodations for players. In another effort to guarantee themselves financial security, the Eastern Band purchased a mirror manufacturing firm in 1987. Although mirrors are not made on Qualla Boundary, the profits from the company will support tribal services.

Eastern and western Cherokees may live in widely different areas of the United States, but they consider themselves one people. Friendships and family ties draw East and West together, and for years Cherokees have traveled hundreds of miles to attend each other's country fairs. In April 1984 a joint council formally met at Red Clay—the site where the Cherokees met when Georgia outlawed their government during the removal crisis of the 1830s—in order to reaffirm the importance of their common heritage.

Cherokees are not merely people of the past: They live in the present and plan for the future. Change and adaptability are a part of their heritage, a persistent theme in their history. When the sons of Kana'ti and Selu could no longer depend on an assured supply of game, they learned to hunt and farm. In meeting the challenges of the 20th century, modern Cherokees are the true heirs of Kana'ti and Selu. Drawing strength and inspiration from the past, they face the future with confidence. The Cherokees are, after all, the Ani'-Yun'wiya, the principal people. ▲

BIBLIOGRAPHY

Brown, Virginia Pound. *The World of the Southern Indians*. Birmingham, AL: Beechwood Books, 1983.

Finger, John R. *The Eastern Band of Cherokees, 1819–1900*. Knoxville: University of Tennessee Press, 1984.

Hicks, Hannah. "The Diary of Hannah Hicks." *American Scene* 13 (1972).

Malone, Henry Thompson. *Cherokees of the Old South: A People in Transition*. Athens: University of Georgia Press, 1956.

Moutlon, Gary E. *John Ross, Cherokee Chief*. Athens: University of Georgia Press, 1985.

Perdue, Theda. "Letters from Brainerd." *Journal of Cherokee Studies* 4 (1979): 4-9.

———. *Nations Remembered: An Oral History of the Five Civilized Tribes, 1865–1907*. Westport, CT: Greenwood, 1980.

———. *Slavery and the Evolution of Cherokee Society, 1540–1866*. Knoxville: University of Tennessee Press, 1979.

Pierce, Earl Boyd, and Rennard Strickland. *The Cherokee People*. Phoenix: Indian Tribal Series, 1973.

Satz, Ronald N. *American Indian Policy in the Jacksonian Era*. Lincoln: University of Nebraska Press, 1975.

Strickland, Rennard. *Fire and the Spirits: Cherokee Law from Clan to Court*. Norman: University of Oklahoma Press, 1982.

Wardell, Morris L. *A Political History of the Cherokee Nation, 1838–1907*. Norman: University of Oklahoma Press, 1938.

White, Anne Terry. *The False Treaty: The Removal of the Cherokee from Georgia*. New York: Scholastic Book Service, 1970.

THE CHEROKEE AT A GLANCE

TRIBE *Cherokee*

CULTURE AREA *Southern Appalachian Mountains*

GEOGRAPHY *Oklahoma, North Carolina*

LINGUISTIC FAMILY *Iroquoian*

CURRENT POPULATION *72,000 in Oklahoma, 8,000 in North Carolina*

FIRST CONTACT *Hernando de Soto, Spanish, 1540*

FEDERAL STATUS *Recognized*

GLOSSARY

acculturation The process by which one culture changes and adapts to the dominant culture it confronts.

allotment A U.S. policy for giving land to Indians, applied nationwide through the General Allotment Act of 1887, intended to bring Indians into the mainstream by breaking up tribally owned reservations and tribal governments. Each tribal member was given, or allotted, a tract of land for farming.

asi Cherokee winter homes of wattle and daub construction with a hearth in the center of the room.

black drink An herbal drink used by tribes throughout the Southeast to induce vomiting as part of a purification ritual.

booger dance A mocking dance performed by the Cherokee to express hostility for their enemies.

Bureau of Indian Affairs (BIA) A U.S. government agency established in 1824 and assigned to the Department of the Interior in 1849. Originally intended to manage trade and other relations with Indians and especially to supervise tribes on reservations, the BIA is now involved in programs that encourage Indians to manage their own affairs and improve their educational opportunities and general social and economic well-being.

clan A multigenerational group having a shared identity, organization, and property, based on belief in descent from a common ancestor. Because clan members consider themselves closely related, marriage within the clan is strictly prohibited. Cherokee clan membership is determined by matrilineal descent.

council house A large village structure in which Cherokee gathered to socialize, debate, and conduct religious ceremonies. Cherokee council houses were of wattle and daub construction.

General Allotment or **Dawes Act** An 1887 federal law that divided reservation land into 160-acre farms granted to individual Indians, who were then required to give up tribal practices and become American citizens.

Green Corn Ceremony An annual celebration of purification, forgiveness, and thanksgiving held when the new crop of corn ripened.

Homestead Act An 1862 federal law that granted 160 acres of land to any head of a family who agreed to cultivate the land for five years.

Indian Removal Act An 1830 federal law that authorized the relocation of eastern Indian tribes to new lands west of the Mississippi River.

Indian Reorganization Act A 1934 federal law that ended the policy of allotting plots of land to individuals and provided for political and economic development of reservation communities.

matrilineal; matrilineality A principle of descent by which kinship is traced through female ancestors; the basis for Cherokee clan membership.

matrilocal residence A tradition in which a newly married couple lives with or near the wife's mother's family.

missionaries Advocates of a particular religion who travel to convert nonbelievers to their faith.

Proclamation of 1763 A royal decree of George III of Britain, it prohibited colonists from settling west of the Appalachian Mountains and reserved this area for Indians.

removal policy A federal policy formulated in 1830 that called for the sale of all Indian land in the states and for the resettlement of Indians from eastern and southern states in segregated western territory (later Kansas and Oklahoma). Those Indians who remained in the East were subject to state laws.

reservation A tract of land set aside by treaty for the occupation and use of Indians; also called a reserve. Some reservations were for an entire tribe; many others were for unaffiliated Indians.

Trail of Tears The harsh journey of Cherokee forced out of their homeland in the Southeast by the federal government to their relocation site in what is now Oklahoma.

treaty A contract negotiated between representatives of the United States and one or more Indian tribes. Treaties dealt with surrender of political independence, peaceful relations, land sales, boundaries, and related matters.

trust land Land set aside and controlled by the U.S. government for use by Indians.

War Woman A woman who traveled with a Cherokee raiding party to cook for them and to organize the camp. Her responsibilities also included taking care of women and children prisoners of war and administering the torture or killing of male prisoners.

INDEX

African slaves. *See* Slaves and slavery

Agriculture. *See* Farming

Allotments, 80–81, 91, 93–94, 97–98. *See also* General Allotment Act

American Board of Commissioners for Foreign Missions, 41–42

American Civil War, 64, 73–78, 80, 85, 86

American Revolution, 35–36, 39, 50

Animals, 18–19, 25, 27, 64, 73, 84; in myth, 13–14. *See also* Bear; Deer; Food; Horses; Hunting

Appalachian Mountains, 13, 35

Appomattox, Virginia, 76

Baptists, 41

Bear, 19

Bear grease, 17, 19

Bingo, 103

Black drink, 22

Black Fox, 52

Blowguns and darts, 19

Boudinot, Elias, 44, 50, 62, 64

Bows and arrows, 14, 19, 31

Brainerd School, 42

Bureau of Indian Affairs. *See* U.S. Bureau of Indian Affairs

Burnett, John G., 58

Ceremonial dances, 18, 28–29, 94

Charleston, South Carolina, 30, 32–33

Chattanooga, Tennessee, 41

Cherokee, North Carolina, 87

Cherokee Advocate, 64

Cherokee Constitution. *See* Constitution of the Cherokee Nation

Cherokee County, North Carolina, 95

Cherokee language and names, 13, 30, 43–45, 64,

93. *See also* Sequoyan syllabary

Cherokee Nation v. Georgia, 56

Cherokee Phoenix, 44, 50, 57, 64

Cherokee Republic, 49

Cherokee Strip, 78, 80

Cherokee Tribal Community Services, 100

Chickamaugas, 36–37

Chickasaw tribe, 22, 28, 34, 55

Child rearing, 16–17, 21, 41–42

Chocktaw tribe, 28, 34, 55, 76

Civil War. *See* American Civil War

Clans, 21. *See also* Kinship system

Cleveland, Grover, 80

Clothing, 18, 32. *See also* Deerskin; Tanning

Coasa River, 45

Collier, John, 98

Compact of 1802, 55

Constitution of 1839. *See* Constitution of the Cherokee Nation

Constitution of the Cherokee Nation, 47, 54–55, 63–64

Constitution of the United States, 47, 49

Cooking, 16–17, 32, 41. *See also* Corn; Food

Corn, 16–17, 25, 27; destruction of crop by British troops, 34–35

Council House, 15, 25

Creek tribe, 22, 28, 55, 74

Curtis Act, 94

Dawes, Henry L., 79

Dawes Act. *See* General Allotment Act

Dawes Commission, 80–81

Death practices, 22, 24

Deer, 18

Deerskins, 18, 30–31, 40. *See also* Trade

Delaware tribe, 77

De Soto, Hernando, 27–28

Disease, 28–30, 35

Drew, John, 74

Eastern Band of Cherokees, 83–91, 95, 97–98, 100–101, 103; as corporation, 89–90

Education, 41–42, 64, 83, 87, 99–100

English language, 46–48

Euchella, 83–84

Family Life, 15, 21. *See also* Clans; Housing; Kinship system; Social organization; Village life

Farming, 16, 24, 27, 103

Farming implements, 30–32, 40

Finger, John R., 99

Fishing, 19

Five Civilized Tribes, 81

Five County Northeastern Oklahoma Cherokee Organization, 101

Food, 16–17, 25. *See also* Cooking; Corn; Fishing; Hunting

Fort Loudon, Tennessee, 33–34

Fort Prince George, South Carolina, 33

Freedmen, 93. *See also* Reconstruction

French and Indian War. *See* Seven Years' War

Gadugi, 87

Gambling, 21, 103

Games, 20. *See also* Stick ball

Gender roles, 16–20, 42, 99

General Allotment Act, 79–81. *See also* Allotments

Georgia Guard, 55

G.I. Bill, 99

Ginseng, 84

Graham County, North Carolina, 95

Grant, James, 34

Grant, Ulysses S., 76

Great Smoky Mountain National Park, 97–99
Great Smoky Mountains, 58, 98
Great Society, 100
Green Corn Ceremony, 25, 94
Guns, 31, 36

Hawkins, Benjamin, 36
Hicks, Hannah, 75
Homeland, 47, 49, 50, 54
Homestead Act, 77–78, 80
Horses, 27, 64
Housing, 15, 18, 25, 30, 73, 100
Hunting, 18–20, 24–25, 27, 31, 103; role of hunters, 32
Hunting grounds, 35, 39–40, 50
Hunting rituals, 25, 88

Indian Emergency Conservation Work Program, 97
Indian Removal Act, 55
Indian Reorganization Act (IRA), 98
Indians Claims Commission, 100
Iroquois tribe, 28, 33

Jackson, Andrew, 55, 57, 59
Jackson County, North Carolina, 95
Jefferson, Thomas, 51, 53, 61
Jewelry, 18
Johnson, Lyndon B., 100
Judicial system, 46

Kàná ti, 13–14, 18, 24, 25, 83, 88, 103
Keeler, W. W., 94
Keetoowah, 94
Kentucky River, 35
Kingfisher, 24
Kinship system, 21, 30
Knoxville, Tennessee, 86

Land and property, 35–37,

39, 47, 49, 51, 55, 64, 77, 79–80, 89–91, 94, 101; land as holy place, 54; land exchanges, 49–59; land values, 77. *See also* Allotments
Laws, 45–47
Lee, Robert E., 76
Lighthorse Guard, 45
Litchfield County, Connecticut, 45
Little Tennessee River, 34, 83–84
Livestock. *See* Animals.
Looms, 40
Louisiana Purchase, 51, 61

Mankiller, Wilma, 101
Marion, Francis, 34
Medicine men and priests, 29–30, 88
Methodists, 41
Miegs, Return J., 40
Mission schools and missionaries, 40–43, 50, 64, 83. *See also* Baptists; Education; Methodists; Moravians
Montgomery, Archibald, 34
Mooney, James, 14, 88
Moravians, 41
Mortar and pestle, 17
Mount Holyoke Female Seminary, 64

National Committee, 47
National Council, 40–47, 54, 74
National party, 61–63
National Youth Administration, 97
Neutral lands, 64, 88
New Deal, 97–98

Oconaluftee Cherokees, 84. *See also* Eastern Band of Cherokees
Oconaluftee River, 84
Oconostota, 33–34
Office of Indian Affairs. *See* U.S. Office of Indian Affairs

Ohio River valley, 33
Oil, 94
Oklahoma Indian Welfare Act, 99
Oklahoma Office of Charities and Corrections, 94
Old Settlers, 61–63
Opothleyohola, 74
Osage, 50
Owen, Robert Latham, 93

Pardo, Juan, 27–28
Path Killer, 52
Philadelphia, Pennsylvania, 75
Plows. *See* Farming Implements
Politics and government, 21, 36–37, 45–47, 54, 55, 79–80
Population, 28, 64, 78
Pottery, 18
Printing press, 43

Quakers. *See* Society of Friends
Qualla Boundary, 95, 97–98, 100, 102–3

Railroads, 77
Reconstruction, 86
Red Clay, Georgia, 103
Reese, Nancy, 42
Religion. *See* Ceremonial dances; Creation myths; Death practices; Hunting rituals; Medicine men and priests; Religious ceremonies; Sacred Formulas; Spirits
Religious ceremonies, 15, 25
Ridge, John, 57, 62
Ridge, Major, 57, 62
Roosevelt, Franklin D., 97–98
Ross, John, 45, 50, 57–59, 61–63
Ross, Lewis, 45
Ross, William P., 64
Rutherford, Griffith, 36

Sacred formulas, 88
Savannah River, 34
Scott, Winfield, 84
Selu, 13–14, 16, 24, 25, 83, 88, 103
Seneca tribe, 22
Sequoyah, 43–44
Sequoyah (proposed state), 81
Sequoyan syllabary, 44–45, 47, 87–88
Seven Years' War, 33, 35–36
Shawnee tribe, 22, 33, 77
Slaves and slavery, 27, 32, 36, 45, 73, 76–77, 86
Smith, Nimrod Jarrett, 89
Smith, Red Bird, 94
Smithsonian Institution, 88
Smoky Mountains. See Great Smoky Mountains
Social organization, 15, 21, 25, 30–31, 36–37, 45–47
Society of Friends, 87
Souvenirs, 98
Spirits, 13, 22, 24, 25, 54
Spring Place, Georgia, 41, 45
Stick ball, 20–21
Stomp ground, 94
Swain County, North Carolina, 95
Swimmer, 88

Tanning, 18
Thomas, William Holland, 84–86
Timber, 90, 96

Tipis, 102
Tools, 17, 36. See also Farming implements; Looms; Mortar and pestle
Tories, 35
Torture, 24
Tourism, 102
Trade and trading, 30–31, 37, 40
Trail of Tears, 57–59, 83
Treaties, 37, 49, 50, 55
Treaty of 1819, 83
Treaty of New Echota, 57, 61
Treaty party, 57, 61–62
Truman, Harry S., 94
Tsali, 84–85
Tuckaseigee River, 34

U. S. Army, 58, 75
U. S. Bureau of Indian Affairs, 99
U. S. Congress, 51, 55, 79–81, 90–91, 95, 99
U. S. Constitution. See Constitution of the United States
U. S. government, 39–40, 43, 45, 49–50, 52, 54–55, 64, 74, 77, 83, 85–87, 90, 98, 100
U. S. Office of Indian Affairs, 63
U. S. Senate, 58, 93
U. S. Supreme Court, 56–57, 88

U. S. Treaty Commission, 57

Van Buren, Martin, 59
Vann, Joseph, 45
Village councils, 21–22, 32; loss of influence, 36
Village life, 14, 21, 25, 27

War and warriors, 22–23, 31–33, 35–37, 39
Warbonnets, 102
Ward, Nancy, 24
War of Independence. See American Revolution
War Women, 24
Washington, D.C., 75, 88
Watie, Stand, 62–63, 74–77
Wattle-and-daub, 15
Wealth and money, 25, 27, 30, 45, 96, 102–3
Wheeler-Howard Act. See Indian Reorganization Act
White Cherokees, 91, 93, 97–98
Wild Boy, 13, 83
Winter house, 15, 18
Witthoft, John, 87, 96, 100
Worcester, Samuel V., 56, 64, 75
Worcester v. Georgia, 56
Works Progress Administration, (WPA), 97
World War I, 90
World War II, 90
Yonaguska, 84–85

PICTURE CREDITS

THEDA PERDUE is professor of history at the University of Kentucky. She is author of *Slavery and the Evolution of Cherokee Society, 1540–1866* (1979) and *Native Carolinians: The Indians of North Carolina* (1985) as well as many articles on southeastern Indians. She has edited *Nations Remembered: An Oral History of the Five Civilized Tribes, 1865–1907* (1980) and *Cherokee Editor: The Writings of Elias Boudinot* (1983). She has been a fellow of the Rockefeller Foundation and the D'Arcy McNickle Center for the History of the American Indian at the Newberry Library.

FRANK W. PORTER III, general editor of INDIANS OF NORTH AMERICA, is director of the Chelsea House Foundation for American Indian Studies. He holds a B.A., M.A., and Ph.D. from the University of Maryland. He has done extensive research concerning the Indians of Maryland and Delaware and is the author of numerous articles on their history, archaeology, geography, and ethnography. He was formerly director of the Maryland Commission on Indian Affairs and American Indian Research and Resource Institute, Gettysburg, Pennsylvania, and he has received grants from the Delaware Humanities Forum, the Maryland Committee for the Humanities, the Ford Foundation, and the National Endowment for the Humanities, among others. Dr. Porter is the author of *The Bureau of Indian Affairs* in the Chelsea House KNOW YOUR GOVERNMENT series.